About the author

Nat Khamphew was born in 1993 in a small village nestled among the thickly forested hills of northern Laos. His parents and grandparents had survived a war that was not theirs, flight into the unknown and resettlement in hostile territory. Largely cut off from the world outside, they continued to live by their Khmu traditions of subsistence farming and animist spirituality. Enjoying the simplest of pleasures and enduring the harshest of circumstances Nat went on to become a Buddhist monk. This is their story and his.

A note on the Khmu

The Khmu are one of the 49 ethnic groups in Laos, with more than 600,000 members, making it the second largest community after the Lao. No one knows exactly from where they came. No evidence or proof indicates that they originated in southern China, as other Lao groups did. The Khmu believe themselves to be indigenous. Some though think they came from the east of India. On a trip to Myanmar in 2017 I came to believe that the Khmu may have came from there, or at least through this area. I visited one of the Burmese tribes near Bagan and to my surprise this group shared many characteristics with Khmu. Skin colour, facial features, house styles, patterns of livestock raising and of bamboo weaving were just as among the Khmu. The language, however, is very different. Perhaps the Khmu came from further west. On a trip to Kathmandu, I was regularly taken to be a native Nepalese. My facial features were common all round me. From oral history the Lao said the Khmu were the first who were brought as slaves into the palace by the Lao monarchy. The Khmu faced discrimination until around 2000. Before that, when a Lao person became angry with a Khmu they would often use the insult 'Ka', a Lao word meaning 'slave'. Nowadays you can still hear this word used among elderly Lao from time to time.

Nat Khamphew

Khmu Cradling

The Private Library
London

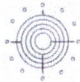

ISBN: 9780956677563

Published by:
The Private Library
15 Pendrell House
New Compton St
London WC2H 8DF, UK
email: rorcal40@hotmail.com

Contents

Introduction

My name is Nat. The name was chosen in an infancy ritual by a shaman, five months after I was born. The word has no meaning.

According to my mother, I was really sick when the shaman came. My Dad had decided to invite him to the house so he could check on my illness while carrying out a blessing at the same time.

During the ceremony the shaman performed magic. He added some herbs and ginger to a glass of water. He sipped from the mixture, then he spurted the contents from his mouth over my head.

On three slips of paper he had written three names. He put each of these inside balls of sticky rice, and placed these on the floor. Then he asked my Mom to hold me closer to the rice balls and allow me to touch one of them, randomly. Whichever I touched would be my name.

Touching the middle ball, I became Nat.

The shaman told my Mom that I'd lost my soul in the stream. This split the path between our house and the farm, and was the one that Mom carried me over, back and forth, each day. This proximity to the stream had caused my sickness, the shaman said. He asked my parents to perform a sacrifice to the spirit who inhabited the area around the stream so that I would recover.

A day later my Dad brought a chicken to the stream. He built a little bamboo spirit shelter. Then he killed the chicken as a sacrifice, and called my soul home. Three or four days later, I recovered.

I was the fifth child in the family. Then, when I was around four years old, my mother gave birth to another daughter and one last girl followed. My parents gave this baby girl away to adoptive parents because they couldn't afford to keep her. Eight months later she died. No-one knew why.

My parents spent most of their time working on the farm. Me and my younger sister were cared for by an older brother and sister. The other older sister and brother helped my parents in the fields.

I was the most troublesome little one in the family, according to my sister. She got spanked by my Dad once when I ate my own poop after she had left me alone for a short time. The spanking was a punishment for not doing her job as a babysitter.

One time, when my Dad was drunk, I cried a lot, and loudly. He nearly shot me with his rifle. My sister grabbed me and carried me away to safety in the woods. Otherwise I might have been dead by the age of four.

1: War

Chapter 1

Orphans of war

My father was called Khamphew. He was given the name at birth. He and his older brother Phou were born during the war. Their father joined the army and never came back. Nobody knew what happened to him.

Their father's wife, my grandmother, was a quiet young woman. She regularly fell ill from an unknown disease.

My father never told us either of their names.

She and her two boys fled their home town. It was in the war zone in the east of the country, a place so badly carpet-bombed that nothing was left of towns like Phonsavanh.

According to Khmu tradition this was where the warrior Kun Jet-jeung had long ago vanquished his enemies. He celebrated this great victory by building hundreds of waist-high rock jars to fill with Khmu rice whiskey. This same Plain of Jars became one of the most bombed locations on the planet.

Khamphew was around 11 years old and Phou 13 as the bombing reached its height. They set off with their mother and two other families. They walked along dirt tracks across two provinces, the thud of carpet bombing receding as they went.

The group was on the move along forest trails for nearly a month, searching for a place where they could settle. Then my grandmother and her boys became separated from the group. The three of them were quite alone in the jungle.

Shortly afterwards, as the sun beat down in the middle of the day, the little party reached a new settlement. Only around 20 families had set up before them so they were among the pioneers. They were not treated as strangers — almost everyone there had fled the bombing.

The place was called Hat Hai, a small refugee community of Khmu people.[1] The villagers welcomed the family group with offers of food and water. One of the families took them in for a few days. Then they built themselves their own bamboo hut with help from their new neighbours.

Their village was deep in the middle of the jungle, but it was also close to a river so it was easy

---

[1] 'Hat Hai' means 'stream of tears'. A long time ago, during a civil war between the tribes, the enemy invaded the village and killed all the men and boys. They left only the women. The smallest boys – two to five years old – were captured and drowned in the stream. Their bodies were washed away by the strong current. The stream was named for them.

for people to farm and fish. Both teenage boys became hard workers because their mother couldn't do the job given her poor health. To feed themselves they grew rice, corn and vegetables.

After nearly three years in their new home the family gave up waiting for their father to return from the war. The village had grown as more arrivals turned up. Everyone was searching for hope and a home. The village became more lively and came to be called Ban Nong Keo.[2]

A year later, when Khamphew was 15, his mother, whose name I never learned, died from her undiagnosed illness. The boys were orphans. Phou worked even harder on the farm to provide for the two of them.

For two more years the two boys lived by themselves. Then Phou met a girl and soon afterwards, when he was about 20, he married her.

---

[2] 'Nong Keo' means 'pond of crystal stone'. In the past its story was passed across the generations. In the middle of the village was a sacred pond where the villagers used to pay their respects. The pool was believed to hold the village's protecting spirit. At full moon, a holy day, a big, round and very beautiful crystal gemstone used to appear in the middle of the night. The villagers could see it. But, as soon as the moon set, the stone disappeared again. The pond no longer exists but the spot where it once was has been left empty. No one dares to build a house on that patch of ground.

Khamphew continued to live with his brother and wife. They loved him and took care of him. When Phou's wife gave birth to their first child my father had to work harder on the farm because his brother had to spend more time at home taking care of his wife and his new-born boy.

Life was good for the four of them.

Chapter 2

In flight

My mother Vanh was born into a quite wealthy family in a small, mixed Christian and Animist village in the south of Luang Prabang province. Her father Peng was expecting a boy. He was a little disappointed.

Peng died soon afterwards, of an unknown illness. Vanh became an only child. Vanh's mother Geud remarried, a man called Ser.

During the holidays some of the villagers used to gather in a small church. Then a man, whom they called 'Father', used to arrive and preach. He talked about God and how he protected his people.

Vanh had a lively childhood. From a young age she used to walk with other children to the main road carrying corn, rice and vegetables. There they could exchange their goods for clothing and candies. But, when she was around 15 years old, her stepfather Ser and other men in the village were forced to join the army. They headed off to fight in the war.

The women and children were left on their own. Soon, when the country was dragged more and more into the conflict, people had to flee from their homes to wherever they thought was safe. My mother and her Mom were among those who had to leave home in search of a new place.

The two of them and two other families decided to migrate northwards while many others scattered in other directions. Some chose to remain in the village. They were waiting for their husbands and fathers to return from the war. One of the families migrating with Vanh was her aunt, Ser's sister Yahern. She had lost her husband through illness. She had a son.

Before they left the village my grandmother buried a big jar full of coins and other valuables in their backyard. They couldn't carry everything. She was hoping to return and find the jar when the situation settled down and they would be able to live there again.

Their journey took them nearly two months. The three families walked through the thick forest on their own, looking for a place they could call home. Along the way they came across many villages but they weren't convinced about settling in any of them.

Then they also arrived at Hat Hai.

Despite being the newest arrivals they felt comfortable remaining because most of the families who lived there were refugees themselves. They spoke the same language and had the same culture. They were all Khmu. My mother felt at home.

My mother and grandmother were offered

shelter and food by the villagers for the first few days. With their own money they hired people to build them a beautiful bamboo hut.

My mother slowly got used to her new home and made some friends. Deep down she still missed her home town and her lively childhood surrounded by friends. She missed her father a lot.

At war

For Ser, the war was horrendous. He was caught up in battle for seven months. He had little sleep, lost his friends, ate wild fruit and snails to survive. He almost starved. Many times the soldiers had to sleep in the middle of heavy downpours. If they were lucky, they found a cave or a big tree where they could shelter from the rain. Setting a fire was rarely allowed because the officers were afraid the enemy would spot the smoke from a distance.

Finally it became too much. Ser, along with three other soldiers, decided to abandon the army. The four of them had had enough so, reluctantly, they were going to run away. They knew the rule that anyone doing so before the war ended would be executed. But, for his part, my grandfather wanted only to return home to his wife and daughter.

That night, they were posted for patrol, four of them keeping an eye on their 17 troops. Around midnight the rain was coming down heavily. In such thick jungle, it was pitch dark. The four young men looked at each other and broke into a run.

The track was slippery. Leeches squirmed. They walked, ran, tripped, walked again. They stumbled on without stopping, terrified of being tracked by their former comrades.

In the morning they reached the edge of the jungle covering. They had come far enough that the other soldiers could not follow. They stopped by a river, rested and washed themselves. They ploughed on for the rest of the day. Finally they found a cave and decided to take a rest and bed down for the night.

Sleeping, my grandfather dreamed he had stepped on cow dung. This was a bad vision in Khmu lore, especially in the midst of war. But next morning, when he told his fellows about the dream, they laughed at him. It's just a dream, one said.

Walking so far and with no food to eat they were exhausted, but they kept on walking. Eventually, they found some wild fruit, sated their hunger and rested.

Then they walked on again, keeping themselves content by thinking of when they would reach home and their families. The leading one of the four stepped on a mine. He was killed instantly. A second was badly injured. Ser suffered a gaping shrapnel wound to his thigh. The fourth, lagging behind everyone else, was unscathed.

The surviving three young men were in shock. They had lost their friend. One of them was seriously injured. They had no medical support, not even a first-aid kit.

They tried to stop their bleeding by applying leaves of, in Khmu, *Jid Keo*, a wild leaf that can stanch a haemorrhage. Soon after, the second young man died from his injuries. He had lost too much blood.

The last two buried their friends in the middle of nowhere.

The pair kept on walking until they came across a small village. Children cried and ran away as they arrived. They thought my grandfather and his friend were the enemy and that they would kill them. My grandfather's friend persuaded them there was no need to be afraid.

The villagers hosted them, giving them food and water. A woman helped Ser with the wound on his thigh, applying a traditional poultice to it. They stayed for several days until they regained some strength. Then they decided to walk on again.

Nearly a month of trekking passed. Finally, they agreed to separate in order to reach their own home towns. Now on his own, Ser took another two days to reach his village. He arrived in the early evening. He quietly headed towards his house. The village was very quiet. It unsettled him.

He reached his old home but the door was closed. He entered and it was bare, abandoned. So much of the family's possessions had been packed away. So much had gone. He sensed that the house had been left like this for quite some time. He became despondent, and pined for his wife and daughter. He wondered if they were alive at all.

The next morning he made his presence known to neighbours. They told him that mother and daughter had left the village for the north, along with two other families, a full eight months before.

Early next morning, Ser packed again and quickly left in search of his family.

The long search

The journey was not easy. Ser had to hide himself as much as he could, especially from the army. He was afraid that he would be caught and sent back to serve again. He could have been executed if they knew he had just fled the military. Every time he approached a village he spent at least an hour reconnoitring, to see if any men were around. Otherwise he wouldn't enter.

Each time he did go in he asked if anyone knew his wife and daughter. He told them their names and where they came from.

Villagers usually served him food and water, and engaged in conversation. Sometimes when people asked him who he was he used a different name, to protect his identity. Some were curious, even suspicious, when they saw him among them instead of being in the army. They all knew that men were being forced to serve in the military.

He walked through village after village, day after day, night after night. He slept whenever he was tired. Often he slept in the forest. Sometimes he was lucky enough to come across someone's farm hut. He would sneak in and snatch a rest.

After several weeks he felt depressed and tired. He didn't give up.

One day he broke into a little farm hut for a rest on the floor. He fell asleep. The next thing he knew, an elderly woman was crying out. The owner of the hut had returned.

When she had opened the door and seen a man laying there asleep she had taken fright at the thought that he was an enemy soldier.

Ser awoke, startled. He quickly told her he was no villain, just a man looking for his wife and daughter. He tried to leave but the woman stopped him. She asked if he were hungry and if he needed some more rest.

He paused. The woman offered him rice and chili paste. They sat. They talked about the war and how it had affected people's lives. How difficult it was to live in such conditions, with people having to flee their homes. So many men had been killed in battle . . .

The woman told him he could stay as long as he wanted. He accepted her offer and stayed for another two days to catch up on rest. The woman continued to bring him food and water.

After leaving the kindly old woman's hut, he travelled on. Six more days later he reached Hat Hai. As usual, he asked if his wife and child might be there.

Only this time the answer was yes. He felt a moment of pure happiness.

He had found his family. And each was so happy. After nearly a year of separation they had found each other again. They were alive.

Yahern

2: Animism

Chapter 3

First love

S er quickly fell in love with his new community and his little family. He and Geud invited his sister Yahern to their house for celebrations and to share stories of good and bad times.

The villagers were hospitable and numerous in this concealed encampment, deep in the jungle. They hunted, gathered wild vegetables and fruit, grew crops and raised cattle. They lived happily. The war ended. The men who'd managed to survive the fighting came back to their families.

The community grew as families formed and new arrivals turned up. Those already there were friendly and always welcomed their new neighbours with snacks, support and food. They often hosted them in their own small homes for a few days or a week until the newcomers were able to build their own bamboo huts.

Ser and Geud built their own big house a few years after arriving. It was one of the first wooden homes in the village, built in the Khmu style up on long stilts, with the upper floor having the bedroom and kitchen. The lower level was left unenclosed so people could sit around in the shade and relax on hot days. Ser made close friends. They all went hunting in the forest together and helped out on each others' farms.

When his stepdaughter Vanh, my mother, was almost 18 years old she was beautiful, with a big, friendly smile. Many young men fell for her.

Young girls then spent most of their day helping their parents in the field because the village had no school. Vanh helped her parents plant and harvest rice, and minded the cows and pigs. She also learned how to weave nets for fishing in the river. Being an only child came with more responsibility. Her stepfather Ser came to admire her when she became such a hard worker.

Some days, when she was not helping her parents in the farm, Vanh and her friends went fishing or collected vegetables or other foodstuffs. Then they prepared meals for their parents in the evening for when they came back from working long hard days in the fields. She was very good at taking responsibility for her chores.

In those times, by the age of 18 a girl was old enough to have her own family. A few guys wanted to get to know Vanh and maybe date her, but she wasn't interested. She still enjoyed living as a single person. Once she married she would not be able to have the same kind of lifestyle. "Marriage comes with responsibility", was what her Mom told her.

As the village grew it gained more access to the outside world. People started to build long-boats for communicating between one village and another. People also used the boats to cross the river to their farms and for fishing.

Mid-November to December was the harvest season so every family was busy with gathering their rice before winter set in. At the same time excitement was high in anticipation of the Khmu New Year festival — especially among the young women and young men.

They worked hard and sold their vegetables and rice so they could buy new clothes for the festival. Some exchanged their rice for new clothing.

One day a merchant, his wife and their son came from another village by boat to sell clothing in Nong Keo. Every family flocked to his riverbank store to check on his wares. The girls were excited about buying their new costumes. Geud and Vanh were among the customers that day.

That afternoon, with the store full of people checking out clothes, the pair were in the corner checking out a skirt when a young man, the merchant's son, approached them. He asked Vanh what kind of clothes she was looking for. Vanh couldn't help but be impressed by how friendly and handsome he was.

When Geud pointed to one of the skirts hanging on the rack the man quickly fetched it, handed it to her and asked her to try it on. She did so, the man checked it over and passed a few compliments. Vanh turned red at the flirtation.

Blushing and shy, Vanh quickly decided to take the skirt. Geud paid and they walked home happily.

Vanh could think of little else other than the boy flirting with her. By late afternoon, as she was husking rice with a mortar, the merchant's son turned up and showed interest in what she was doing. They talked a little, and Vanh got to know him a little bit. Before he left he told her that he would return in time for the New Year celebration.

A month later and everyone was excitedly anticipating New Year. Each family saved what little money they had in a box until finally they had enough to buy a water buffalo. Then they invited their neighbours to join them for festivities, with the centre piece being the buffalo for the guests.

The girls and women dressed up in traditional costume, cooked soup, stew, chili paste and dessert while the men built a bamboo stage for dancing.

As the festival started the merchant's son showed up, just as he had said he would. He had dressed up nicely and neatly to impress the girls, especially Vanh.

Music began and soon an announcer asked all the village girls to come forward and sit around the stage. Any men who wanted to dance had to drop money in a jar. This was a donation for the village that would be used later to build a hall or a school.

Vanh was sitting round the stage with the other girls when suddenly she heard her name called by the DJ. He asked her to come up to dance. Her dancing partner would be the merchant's son. Feeling shy and excited in equal measure it was an honour to be called up first. Then two others were called and their three suitors joined them. The girls placed a wreath of flowers around each boy's neck as a sign of gratitude and appreciation for their donation. Then they danced, with all the villagers looking on.

After the festival the merchant's boy came to the village once every 10 days to meet with Vanh and her family. Many times her parents invited him and his family to their house for a meal and a drink. The parents of both sides liked each other very much.

But as the relationship deepened Vanh found herself not feeling so sure. He asked for her hand in marriage, but she turned him down. Geud and Ser were disappointed because they'd found a young man with corresponding wealth status for their daughter. It was common for parents to want the most for their girls, and girls often chose men based on status — but not Vanh.

Love from a distance

Khamphew was around 21 then, exceptionally tall. You could see his hairy legs from a distance. His pale skin also made him stand out.

He was rather quiet and spent most of his time alone. The past weighed on him. His Dad had gone off to war to join the army but went missing, never to reappear. He had to flee as a refugee from the war zone. His mother died when he was a teenager. He was left alone with his brother, his parents gone, and had to work very hard to provide for himself and his brother's family.

Now he was a grown man, old enough to have his own family. However, being an orphan and of lower status he was very shy about approaching girls. He said once that he felt without value because of his status. He was deeply insecure.

One of the problems was that, in order to find himself a wife, a man had to have money to afford a dowry as well as gifts for the woman's parents. The tradition was that the man's family had to pay the dowry to them. It could be cash, pieces of gold, or an animal such as a water buffalo or cow, or several pigs. Khamphew had none of these.

Not every woman thought money was the priority when looking for a future husband. They looked at the man's behaviour: was he diligent and hard working? Some women looked at these aspects of someone's personality and reckoned if these instead might provide the makings of a good husband and a good father of their children. If the answer was yes then the dowry could be left for future discussions. Being rich was a bonus.

Khamphew had spotted Vanh many times — it's a small village. He knew that he felt something for her but he didn't dare approach. For quite some time he watched Vanh without her realising.

One evening, the weather was cold so people came out together. They set a big fire and sat around to tell stories. It was a clear, starlit night. Many more young men and girls emerged to warm themselves and listen to the entertaining tales, usually about ghosts and evil spirits visiting the village.Some brought sticky rice to make cake and some brought potatoes to grill. The moon was bright as the villagers talked and laughed.

The boys sat on one side and girls on the other. They took turns in telling a story. And, while one of the boys was telling his tale, Vanh noticed Khamphew casting a glance at her. She looked away, then back at him, then away again. At first she didn't think much of it, but finally her curiosity was piqued as Khamphew gazed at her. She brazenly asked him to tell his story. As shy as he was he did his best, and related a tale.

As the fire died down people slowly separated to go back to sleep. Only a few still enjoyed the warmth of the embers, Vanh and Khamphew among them. Vanh could tell that this man was shy, so she decided to talk to him first. And they spoke until nearly midnight. When finally they decided to leave Khamphew asked to walk her back to her home and she accepted his offer. They walked quietly to her house. He said goodbye to her there and walked back to his.

A forbidden relationship

Vanh and Khamphew started seeing each other regularly, but quietly and without others knowing. As the relationship became more serious, she was afraid her parents wouldn't approve.

One evening after dinner she decided to tell them about her love. At first they did not take it seriously. They thought it wouldn't last long. However, Ser did ask if they'd slept together. Traditionally, a boy and girl are not supposed to sleep together before the marriage. If they do, the man is fined. In the most serious cases they have to get married or are forced into marriage.

When Vanh said 'no' they suggested that it would be better not to see him again. Vanh didn't tell this to Khamphew though. She secretly saw him every once in a while.

He knew it wasn't going to be possible for them to be together, so he decided to stay away. However, because they lived in such a small village, trying to avoid one another wasn't much help. They decided to get back together again.

This time Khamphew deliberately showed in public that he had been seeing Vanh. The consequences were not good. When her parents found out about their renewed relationship she faced a big problem. Her parents locked her inside the house for nearly a whole day without food. It was her punishment for not listening to them.

One evening she said to Khamphew: "If you really like me and you want me to be your future wife, you maybe have to do something to prove to my parents that you're the right man for their daughter. So they don't have to worry about me." Being an only child her parents were particularly fond of her and perhaps even over-concerned about her future. As they put it to her once: "If you were a boy we wouldn't have to worry about your future this much."

What they worried about most was, when they

died, whether their daughter would be in good hands. When her parents looked at Khamphew they did not see him as a stable or secure sort. They didn't think he was the right one. His status and his insecurity certainly didn't help. Ser and Geud forbade Vanh from seeing him again.

Persuasion

They were in a pickle, with her parents refusing to let them see each other. Back then a girl getting into a relationship was not easy as it was the parents who usually chose the man for her.

Because they both didn't want to give up on one another Khamphew asked for advice from his brother and sister-in-law. Phou gave the same advice as Vanh had given him: "Show them what you have and what you're good at. Prove to them that you're the right one for her and that you will be a good husband in the future. Show them this and, if they still reject you, then it will be time to give up."

Khamphew talked to Vanh and said he was ready to do anything to let her parents see he was good enough for their daughter. She suggested he should go help them in the farm – just show up there, work and try to talk to them.

Days went by and Khamphew worked harder. He started to go hunting and when he returned successfully he shared the fresh meat, maybe snake, deer or small mammals, with Vanh's family. He showed up at the farm and helped her parents with difficult work such as building a hut, chopping wood and herding cattle when it rained. Sometimes he spent the whole night at their farm to protect the crops from wild animals. On a good night he caught wild boar and he cooked up the meat for them.

Phou and his sister-in-law were happy to see him turn into a more responsible man.

For her part, Vanh did something similar. She woke up early, cooked and prepared meals and did almost all the chores. She worked hard on the farm.

Days turned into months and slowly Ser and Geud started to like Khamphew. They talked more and sometimes Ser and Khamphew went out hunting together. Vanh and Geud would prepare a meal for when they returned.

Finally, the parents told Khamphew that if he was ready to take their daughter as his wife then he should ask his brother and sister-in-law to come talk to them. In Khmu culture the older adults discuss the matter of marriage and engagement of a future young couple. So a man's parents come talk to the woman's family once the relationship has been approved by the family. The negotiations come after the two young people say they are ready to get married. The parents then come and talk about a dowry, what should be provided for the woman's family and what is a good length for the engagement. As Khamphew didn't have surviving parents his brother and sister-in-law stepped in.

Her parents didn't ask for a dowry because they knew Vanh's suitor didn't have it, but they asked him to provide gifts as part of the traditional ceremony in their honour.

This ceremony duly followed and during it Khamphew and his family brought their gifts, marching from his house to Vanh's along with other villagers who wanted to wish them a happy marriage. The gifts were a jar, a chicken and a silver plate.

Her parents ended up paying for the full cost of the ceremony. They killed a cow for the guests, and the whole village was invited. This was an unusual case when the woman's family spent their own wealth on the costs of the wedding. Normally it is the man's responsibility, but Khamphew couldn't afford it.

The ceremony was cheerful and full of joy. The families organised a Baci blessing ceremony with the shaman to bring luck to the new couple. Everyone gossiped at length, laughed and drank too much Khmu whiskey from big jars.

Shaman's altar

Chapter 4

An animist family

Traditionally a newly wed couple have to stay in the woman's family home for at least seven days. Then they decide whether they should move out. In this way they show respect to the woman's parents, and they help out with some of the hard work.

Khamphew and Vanh stayed with her parents for three months before deciding to move into their own little bamboo hut. They still returned to help out from time to time though. But Khamphew didn't feel comfortable, partly because his mother-in-law Geud still looked down on him.

They were given two pieces of land to farm and two cows to start off their new lives.

That year wasn't as good as the previous one because wild animals preyed on them. Boars in particular ate their rice and other crops. Khamphew, with his father-in-law's help, worked hard to build a fence around his own farm and that of Vanh's parents. He spent night after night without proper sleep watching over the farm. He regularly shot boar.

Yet by the time the harvest came, almost half of the rice in the fields had gone. It was not just their families but the rest of the village too. Those with big families began to panic with the fear of not having enough rice to feed themselves. The next harvest would not arrive for another year. Men took to hunting and cutting trees as lumber to sell to merchants from villages along the main road.

Khamphew and Phou were among those who had to do extra jobs to provide for their families. They mostly went hunting rather than felling trees. Sometimes they spent days and nights in the forest, sleeping in caves. They shot large animals, dried the meat, packed it and continued on hunting until they reached their capacity. Finally they came home with loads of meat, including deer, boar, buffalo and squirrel, and sometimes even a tiger. The food they garnered on one expedition could feed them for a month or more. They sold some to merchants and shared some with their neighbours. And of course, some went to Vanh's parents.

Seven months later she became pregnant. She worked on as normal until her belly was so big it became difficult to walk the long path back and forth to the farm. She took to staying mostly at home, and cooked and did the chores while her young husband worked on his own. Sometimes Ser helped him out.

Geud was happy anticipating her first grandchild. She invited Khamphew and Vanh into their spacious house and cooked big meals. They all ate together. Sometimes Phou and his family also joined in. They slowly turned into a happy family.

Vanh gave birth to her first child, and it was a girl. Khamphew was a bit disappointed because he had been hoping for a boy, but he was still very happy. Her parents were the happiest of all because they could take care of Vanh and the new baby so much. On account of bearing a child Vanh was not allowed to eat any food for the first month except rice and grilled salt, with hot water. Villagers were afraid all new mothers might fall ill at a vulnerable time.

Their Animist beliefs played a part in this. A woman who had just given birth was meant to spend most of her time around a lit stove because the villagers believed that the fire protected her and her child from evil spirits. The baby couldn't be left or a spirit might come and play with them and take their soul away. The baby might then fall ill and, sometimes, die as a result of being left alone in the company of the spirit.

Both mother and baby happily survived however, and when the baby turned a month old her parents organised a Baci ceremony for her, as a blessing and to bring her good luck in life. They invited the shaman to come and perform the ritual and to name her. They called her Meuan.

Sacrifice

By mid-July rainy season was in full spate. People were busy tending their crops and rice in the fields.

Khamphew and Ser were exceptionally busy because Vanh and Geud couldn't work as much as normal because of the baby.

With the rain the grass had grown a lot in their fields, so much so that it was smothering the rice and other crops. To save their harvest they asked for help. Many of the villagers came to their aid. But this was on condition that next time they themselves would help out another family and that family in turn would help out another, until a full round was completed.

With the crops saved, it was time for the ceremony of sacrifice, the annual festival to celebrate a successful harvest and to implore the spirits for a successful planting season.

The entire village put enough money together to buy a water buffalo. Then they had a meeting to plan for the big event. They would have to invite at least five shamans to perform the proper rituals over the sacrificial animal. Two were available in the village so they had to find another three from elsewhere. Two men, Ser and another, were sent on this mission to find and bring back the shamans. So they walked for two days to a village called Ban Houy Lae. This other Khmu settlement had three priests so their complement would be complete and they turned for home.

Soon after their return, everyone gathered in Nong Keo, each dressed in traditional costume and head bands. The five shamans, bare-chested with black trousers, a red head band and a sword each, led the way in panathenaic-like procession from the town to a towering tree at the western end of the settlement. Behind the five shamans, five women carried bowls filled with water buffalo's blood. Behind them five men carried bamboo baskets bearing buffalo parts such as horn, feet and tail.

At the tree the spirit shelter lay.

Beneath the spreading branches the shamans prayed. They placed the five bowls of blood and five baskets of meat on the spirit shelter. Their leader incanted a magic spell, an invitation to the spirit to come and witness the ceremony. The buffalo's uncooked blood and intestines were placed inside the shelter as invitation to the spirit to eat and drink while the shamans chanted in their secret language. Then the villagers took their turn in their imprecations, asking for a blessing for their families and for the success of their crops. Then the villagers built a large fire by the tree, cooked the sacrifice and, led by the shamans, feasted on the buffalo meat under the great tree.

With the ceremony completed, everyone paraded back into the village. Once inside, they closed the four gates, to the east, west, south and north. Khmu believe every place has its own spirit. Each village has four gates so its protecting spirit can guard each side as well as the village within from the harm that might come from black magic and evil spirits outside. Beyond, every river, mature tree, boulder and mountain has its own protector.

Once within, the villagers are not allowed to leave and anyone outside was not allowed to enter, for a full day. But now it was time to celebrate — they played games, threw water at each other, laughed a lot, ate a lot and drank homemade liquor.

Nong Keo's particular ceremony of sacrifice has a centuries-old tradition. Its inhabitants believe that a nearby village had been hidden by a spirit. When a tribal war had engulfed the area, the villagers had made a human sacrifice to protect themselves. A widow was offered up to the spirit.

Many times since then, on the day of the holiday, the people of Nong Keo can hear the sound of roosters and children crying nearby. Yet they can never see them. They are the cries of the village that had been hidden by the spirit, forever.

Dreams

Khmu are superstitious. They believe dreams can be interpreted to foretell the near future.

Shamans say dreams are either lucky or unlucky. Lucky dreams are those for which everyone wishes when they close their eyes at night. Even when what happens doesn't turn out how the sleeper's dream predicted Khmu people still return to believing strongly in them because of a need to find comfort. It's a mental trick they use simply to endure.

The lucky dreams for which most Khmu wish are many. Ironically, they long to dream of waking up with a poop stain — that means they'll make their fortune.

A dream of a chicken laying eggs means good luck is on their side and their wishes will be fulfilled.

A dream of crying means they're going to have a better day tomorrow, full of joy and happiness.

One of giving birth means their crops will

bloom, and of picking a flower that a man will meet his soulmate soon.

On the other hand, dreams can be about things for which no-one would wish:

Killing a buffalo signifies losing someone, meaning a family member or villager will die. The killer represents a hungry ghost while the buffalo is an ill human.

A house collapsing means the dreamer will lose a senior family member — father or mother.

A fire means they will argue with someone and it will end in hatred.

Losing a tooth means a family member will die.

Singing or laughing means sorrow will arrive either through death or indeed from any trouble that causes unhappiness.

Beautifying the body, possibly with make-up, mens the person will soon fall ill.

These dreams often result with the shaman being involved and an animal sacrificed to forestall the outcome. Because such dreams are believed so strongly, along with the shamans interpretations, people do whatever it takes to prevent the outcome. Many lose their wealth to the shamans and end up owing their neighbours money.

Recovering Meuan's spirit

When Meuan was a year and two months old she became very sick from an unknown cause. Her parents tried hard to help her with traditional medicine. They didn't talk about hospital. Khmu are conservative in their beliefs. They cured the sick using traditional remedies, and also invited shamans to perform ceremonies and rituals.

After a month the baby was still sick so Geud invited the shaman to come and check what was wrong. He told her that the baby had lost her soul to an evil spirit near the mountain on the way to their farmland. She might die if they did not redeem her soul. He suggested that, in order to redeem her soul from the spirit, my family had to sacrifice a cow, some coins and her clothes to the spirit. Whatever it took, Geud was not going to lose her grandchild so she talked to Ser and decided to sacrifice one of their cows.

The ceremony was long. Two shamans came and helped Geud and Ser to prepare. Many elderly men came to help with the killing of the cow. Khamphew helped them build a spirit house with bamboo in which to place the blood, the cow's meat and the baby's belongings. When the time came the two shamans donned their special clothes with red headbands, as a symbol of power. Each of them carried their own long sword.

Vanh held the baby close to the shamans. They prayed and swung their swords over Meuan as a threat to the evil spirit to return her soul. They wrote her name on a piece of paper and, along with a glass of cow's blood, some meat, her clothing, and 15 silver coins, placed them in the basket. They headed in procession towards a mountain the shaman had nominated. One priest led the troupe and the other followed at the back, so as to protect the people on their way. At the spirit house, they placed their belongings. The shamans performed a ritual, then they all processed back home.

An anxious week passed and the baby slowly began to improve.

More children

A year passed. Vanh's family expanded when a second child was born. Another girl. Khamphew wasn't happy because he wanted a boy but, whatever the baby was, he had to accept it. This fat little girl was healthy. They called her Heuan, a name given by Geud, although she later became known as Lae. She had Khamphew's looks, with big eyes, pale skin and red cheeks that melted her grandmother's heart.

When Heuan turned two months old her grandparents became concerned because now Vanh had two children to take care of and she also had to help Khamphew with work on the farm. They invited her and her family to come and live with them in their big house. It made life a lot easier because now Geud didn't have to walk back and forth to visit her grandchildren. Khamphew wasn't as enthusiastic about the offer but Vanh wanted it, so they moved a week later. Now they were living together as one big family.

A year later, where before they had separate farms, now they had only one, but larger. Geud had become a full-time babysitter at home, while her daughter and son-in-law worked a lot in the fields. Geud helped them sometimes but mostly she prepared food for the days outside. The children grew up fast and healthily. When Meuan was three and a half years old Vanh gave birth to their third child, a boy, and named him Sone. Khamphew was delighted he finally had a boy and his grandparents were happy to have their first grandson.

Khamphew worked harder to provide for the family. He hunted at night and worked in the field during the day and then came home and took care of the family. He was a good father and husband. His parents-in-law liked him. Geud told Vanh: "You've chosen the right man for you and your children."

Yahern adopts a child

Yahern's son had also grown up; he married a girl from the village, moved out and built his family their own separate bamboo hut. But, although they visited often, Yahern felt lonely and in need of someone to help with chores and accompany her to the farm. She talked to her brother Ser to see if he could help by talking to a widow whose husband had recently died from an unknown illness.

The lady had four children: two boys and two girls. She herself had to work hard on the farm to provide for them all. Sometimes they were starving and only had forest potatoes, or other wild vegetables, and bamboo soup to eat. Since they lived not far from Yahern she often saw the girls pass her house with water from the river in dirty, ragged clothes.

Sometimes she would stop them and offer rice and corn, and in return they helped her with chores, such as fetching her water from the river or feeding the pigs and chicken. Sometimes they came to pick long beans and harvest peanuts on Yahern's farm, with Lae usually joining them. In return Yahern always rewarded them with a bag full of food for their family. Lae also returned with a bag full of vegetables and fruit.

When Ser and Yahern talked to the widow about adopting one of her children she was pleased to hear it. She knew that her child would be taken good care of by this kind and generous lady. She herself would have one less mouth to feed. And they were close by so they would still see each other.

After the discussion the widow decided to give her youngest daughter up for adoption. She was 8 years old at the time. Her name was Lid.

Next day Lid packed her bag and clothes and brought them to her new home with the help of her big sister and Lae. The three of them became close friends.

Having the little girl was a blessing for Yahern. She took care of Lid like her own daughter, and not just her but also the girl's family by also providing food and rice for them whenever she could. Often Lid's big sister and Lae spent the night at Yahern's house and woke up early to do the chores before they came back to their own homes.

In those days it was unusual for anyone to live alone. Some other member of the family was always present; if not children it would be grandchildren, or the individual had to adopt some. Adoption wasn't complicated because of the trust people had in each other. It was a win-win situation for both families.

Chapter 5

Tragedy and joy

K hamphew's only brother Phou and his family celebrated when they had their fifth child, a boy they called Ang. But he had reached only two months when Phou became seriously unwell, with an unknown illness. Shortly afterwards, he died.

His wife, who came to be known as YaPhou or Madame Phou, and her five children plunged into a great sadness, Khamphew too. His brother was the only person he had in his life who had linked him to his painful, displaced childhood. Even Phou was gone now.

But, dire as this predicament was, Khamphew and all the family had no option but to accept their grievous situation.

Four of the children were still very young. They couldn't fend for themselves yet. Only the first son Pa was old enough to help his mother with hard work.

In Khmu culture, if someone dies in the village

no one is allowed to make noise, or to leave the settlement for a day. Everyone has to stay put. People come to the family suffering the loss to offer rice and pay their respects to the dead person and join in mourning.

The family then memorialises the day their loved one died, instituting it as a holiday for the family until they too all pass away. In the Khmu calendar, each week has 10 days. So if someone dies on the third day of the week the family keeps that day as their family holiday. On this day the family stays at home. No one is allowed to make noise, and all the windows and doors are left open in the belief that the spirit of the dead person might visit. In the evening the mother prepares food and rice, places it on banana leaves and brings the package to the cemetery so the spirit will come and eat the offering. When someone in the family then falls ill, the sickness is caused by the dead person's spirit. Ceremonies are carried out that involve preparing food or sacrificing animals. The family might also invite a shaman to perform a ritual.

Phou's funeral was simple. His corpse was left undisturbed for two days. Then, before taking the body to the cemetery, the family wrapped it in a mat along with his belongings. These had to be torn or cut as a sign to remind the spirit that Phou was no longer living in the same world as his family.

Whatever world their lost loved ones belong to, Khmu people believe in a reunion. In Phou's case the family believed he would be reunited with his parents somewhere in the spirit world. Perhaps, they thought too, it would only be with his mother.

Nobody knew what had happened to his father when he had gone missing after joining the army during the war.

As dawn broke, Khamphew went on his own into the forest to cut a long log from which they could carry his brother's coffin. The timber had to be fresh and not dried out. Otherwise the corpse would return in evil form.

As Khamphew sorrowfully chopped into the wood with his axe, from behind he heard someone call his name. He mumbled a response. When he turned round no one was there. Fear gripped him. He quickly finished cutting the log and hurried home.

The corpse was wrapped tightly. They put three hooks at the front, middle and end of the mat. Then they hung the hooks from the log that my father had cut in the forest. My father and another man hired for the task lifted the weight onto their shoulders and steadied themselves for the long walk. Many elderly village men and a shaman joined the procession. They carried the corpse to the cemetery — quite far from the village and deep in the forest. Phou's oldest son, though still young, carried a bamboo basket filled with his father's belonging as well as a live chicken.

The moment they entered the environs of the cemetery Khamphew felt the burden weigh much more heavily on his shoulders. Hungry ghosts were climbing into the mat to nourish themselves on the human remains.

The villagers dug a hole as deep as possible. The eldest son Pa had to drop down into it to dig out the last shovelfuls of earth. Emerging, they then let the body down inside the hole and buried Phou along with his belongings. They tied the chicken to a stick next to his grave with a long string so the tethered bird could roam some distance. The chicken was there to accompany the spirit on what would otherwise be a solitary spirit journey.

The shaman performed a ceremony. Then they all walked back home.

For the first three days after the death neighbours have to come to stay with the family so they do not become fearful. The mother, accompanied by a companion, has to bring food and water to the cemetery.

Khmu people believe that, three days after passing away, the dead person won't realise he or she has died. Their spirit will come to visit their family at midnight. For the spirits this is daytime, the time to be with the family as they always had been when they were alive. Some come back because they don't accept at all that they have died. They believe their beloved family still needs them. Then they keep coming back until they are able to accept their death. Finally, they depart for their world, where they belong.

Every time someone dies, the shaman makes protective symbols and places them on steps and doors. A protecting symbol can be a thorn or a sword, sprinkled with holy water, to stop the dead person's spirit from entering the house and frightening the family. When the spirit doesn't realise that he or she has died or doesn't accept they are dead they can be aggressive. They appear in the darkness, their features streaked with blood, their hair long and matted, their faces terrifying.

Khamphew told Vanh about what he had heard as he cut the wood. She became angry and concerned. If a Khmu hears their name being called from a distance, they must not immediately answer. The person must wait until the third call or until they see who is calling. It could be an evil spirit. The spirit, by calling someone's name and receiving a response, will take that person's soul away. Illness and death can follow unless the victim can redeem their soul.

So the family organised a ceremony to stop Khamphew falling seriously ill or dying.

The cost of responsibility

"Losing a father is like losing hope" is a Khmu maxim. The father takes care of everyone, works on the farm, goes hunting and provides for the family in whatever way he can. Hope dies with his passing, especially if his children are young and unable to provide for themselves.

Khamphew and Vanh helped Phou's five children as much as they could. Khamphew worked on their farm, provided food and taught them how to do the many chores around the home and land, especially Pa. He went hunting with Khamphew from time to time, until he knew how to hunt himself.

Vanh tried her best on their behalf too, cooking and bringing food, such as vegetables, bamboo soup, or meat and fish that Khamphew caught. Sometimes her parents invited the whole family for a meal at their house.

YaPhou was kept busy taking care of her new-born boy. The in-between children started to set traps to catch mice and birds for their meals. Sometimes they picked wild vegetables in the forest. They helped with chores and looked after their baby brother too.

A year passed and their situation improved. Slowly the children became used to living without their father. Their mother returned to work as normal, having the younger sister take care of the baby at the farm hut while she and the girls' brothers were working in the fields.

Meanwhile, Vanh gave birth to another boy, called Nid. Her parents were growing older and mostly stayed at home, taking care of the grandchildren and preparing food for Vanh and Khamphew.

Meuan was now old enough to take care of her younger brothers while her parents were out working on the farm.

Khamphew was becoming stressed though with his family responsibilities and by having to face so much work. He started drinking.

I arrive

The situation deteriorated quickly. Nearly a year later Khamphew told Vanh that he didn't want any more children, but they had no contraception at that time. Geud procured Vanh some traditional medicine but it didn't work. Soon Vanh had fallen pregnant again. This time with me.

Khamphew was upset. He kept on drinking and becoming drunk. He came home stressed and became violent.

Geud and Ser didn't feel comfortable. Sometimes they told him to stop drinking, that he should take care of his family. "But I am the one who takes care of the family," he shouted back, "so don't you dare tell me what to do!"

I was born, and soon afterwards he kicked them out of the house, their own house. They built their own bamboo hut on the edge of the village.

They were powerless to stop Dad from his alcoholism and violence. So was Mom. He still worked hard to provide for the family but his anger had become uncontrollable. Sometimes he came home drunk and beat up Mom, then his children. The children became used to running to their grandparents' hut. They felt safe there.

Sometimes they spent the night with their grandparents, leaving only my parents and me, the baby, at home. Every time I cried at night Dad became angry. He threatened Mom that he would kill me if she couldn't stop me crying.

Another bereavement

As the violence within the family deteriorated, everyone felt the disruption. From being a happy family ours became chaotic and frustrated. The children were left on their own. My Mom was busy taking care of me.

My sisters worked harder than ever. Sometimes they had to go to the farm alone and work all day before coming home with vegetables and bamboo shoots. They cooked and provided for their younger siblings. Some evenings they had a meal in their grandparents' place then they would come home, clean up, help Mom bathe me and put me to bed.

During the harvest season I turned a year old. Villagers were busy bringing in their rice and other crops. Geud fell ill so Ser had to spend most of his time taking care of her. Sometimes he had to help Mom and my sisters harvest the rice because Dad was drinking heavily by then and didn't do the job.

One day they all left for the farm. Only me and one of my sisters were left with our ill grandma. Around noon my sister had fed me and put me to sleep. She cooked some food and went to wake Geud for her lunch. But she didn't move. My sister froze in horror, then she leaped from the house and called for help from the nearest neighbours. They came, but Grandma had died.

Two men ran up to the farm to tell my family the news. They all came running home. Everyone cried. Geud's loss brought huge sadness to us all, especially Ser. Alone and angry, he took to complaining more about Dad's behaviour and how it was causing so much unrest. Mom became depressed, frustrated with all the children who needed to be taken care of, and forced to cope with an alcoholic and violent husband.

A week after Geud passed away Mom fell seriously ill from food poisoning for several days. She nearly died. She couldn't feed me with her own milk so every day my sister had to carry me around the village asking the women if they would mind feeding me with their milk. One woman, called Silee, in particular fed me until my Mom recovered.

As time passed Ser became more subdued and morose. He spent most of his time alone. He didn't talk to Mom for a while. His grandchildren couldn't do much to comfort him apart from visiting him with food from time to time.

A year passed. Dad's drinking slowly improved.

Grandfather moves on

As I grew up I cried a lot. And every time I cried Ser would carry me down to the river. There he would jump into his boat. And I would stop crying.

It was another bad harvest year. Once again the whole village was faced with starvation. Many men went to villages nearby to work and to buy rice for their families.

Ser was lonely and sad after losing his wife. He decided to leave us. At first he told us that he would find work and send us some rice. But we never heard from him after that.

Soon afterwards we heard that he had found a woman with whom to live with and to marry, and he was living in a new village. But he never returned to visit us. Communications were not easy in those days. You might have to walk for days to reach your destination if you had some news or important things to do.

Our family was close to starvation. My Mom and sisters scrabbled for wild potatoes and cooked bamboo shoots. We ate them instead of rice. Sometimes we ate just vegetables. Sometimes Dad caught big animals out hunting and we could eat the meat. I was just over two years old.

With the shortage of food I became the weakest child in the family. I was sick very often. As I grew I found it difficult to walk properly. My Mom worried about my lack of nutrition.

The family fell into chaos. Many times my mother had to leave me with my sisters at home while she worked all day on the farm. She only came back in the evening. My sisters could only feed me boiled rice and water. Mom was right – there wasn't much nutrition.

But a difficult year slowly passed and a new, better year started. Dad finally returned to normal. He worked hard to provide for us. We no longer talked about our absent grandfather. It seemed like we were a happy family again.

Falang! Falang!

It was a sunny morning with blue skies. Mom and my brothers and sisters left for the farm leaving me at home alone. Mom had asked me to put the rice out to dry while I was waiting. I had my breakfast and started to load the rice bit by bit since I couldn't carry a whole bag.

Suddenly I heard kids screaming, crying at the tops of their voices "Falang! Falang!"

In the colonial era this word referred to French people. This was because in the Lao language the word 'France' is difficult to pronounce. Lao has neither 'r' nor 's' consonants so r becomes al, and ce, or s, becomes ng. So 'Frans' became 'Falang' and, gradually, we came to use it to denote all white people. Essentially, it meant foreigner.

On hearing the kids crying I ran outside to see what was the matter. The children were running hither and thither, calling in panic for their Moms and Dads. My heart beat faster. Something serious was happening.

We had unexpected visitors — Americans! A group of soldiers had come. The kids cried: "Run! Run! Or they'll take you away!"

But we had nothing to worry about. The soldiers had two guides who reassured the adults that they would do no harm. One asked if they could take him to the village chief.

Soon we kids crept back. We peered at them. They looked like aliens. Big, tall, white skin. And creepy hairstyles, curly and blond.

Some of the aliens smiled. We squealed in terror.

The guides explained that these were army men from the USA and they had come to get rid of unexploded bombs. The bombs had originally been dropped during the American, or Vietnam, war when millions of shells, many of them cluster munitions, were dropped and tens of thousands of Lao had been killed. Decades later, the farmland is still littered with millions of tiny bomblets, or bombies. Half-buried across rice fields and forests, they keep on killing people, even today.

The soldiers explained how dangerous their country's old bombs could be and how we could avoid getting ourselves killed or injured. They explained that most people are struck today as they dig foundations for their huts or hoe the ground for bamboo shoots. They just tap a little bomb, it explodes, and they are killed. More often they lose an arm or a leg, or are blinded for life.

The Americans spent several days clearing their old ordnance. We weren't allowed to go out those days. Almost every hour we would hear a sharp explosion as the soldiers destroyed a device in a controlled way. Wide-eyed and wondering at the violence of it all in our isolated village, chosen because it was as far away as possible from the war and its attendant rain of destruction, we were petrified.

Later I learned that Laos was the most bombed country in the world per head of population. Strange, considering we were never at war with America. I could only imagine what life was like back then, 20 years before I was born

My Mom and Dad had survived it. Somehow.

Hunting with Dad

When I was nearly 6 years old Dad brought me with him when he went out hunting at night. He wanted me to learn and understand how to spot animals and to track them. The first time I trotted after him into the forest. I was barefoot and wearing only my little T-shirt. My only other piece of clothing in the world was a long-sleeved shirt which I left at home.

As night came on I became very scared. It was dark and cold. Dad built a small hut using banana leaves to cover us. Then he went out spotting. I waited for him there alone.

Soon I heard the sound of a gunshot. Dad reappeared and he was carrying a huge deer!

He rested for a bit and then went out again. Soon after there was another gunshot. And another. He came back with another big deer.

Then he crept under the banana leaves beside me and we slept, the night sounds of the jungle all around us. At times like this, curled up beside him, I felt safe with my Dad, the hunter.

When it was almost dawn we decided to go back to our farm hut. It was cold and wet because of the early mist. The moonlight was bright enough for us to walk home comfortably.

Dad carried his pair of deer and, barefoot and brave now, I carried his rifle and the bag.

We got to the hut as the new day began. My Mom and sister were pleased. They cut, sliced and dried the meat. We cooked a big meal and all ate together. Then I went to have a nap and woke to the sounds of the nearby forest.

In the evening Lae and Mom went back to the village. They brought some venison with them, giving some to Phou's children and some to my grandaunt's family. They were also able to exchange it for salt and other kitchen materials.

My Dad continued to bring me hunting with him. I slowly got used to living in the wild and to develop an instinct for the wilderness.

It was so peaceful living in the jungle. Snug under banana leaves in my T-shirt, my Dad's breathing reminding me of his presence, I drifted off to the sound of the animals and woke to the sound of birds singing. The smell from the rice we boiled on the newly kindled fire was fresh and beautiful.

My Dad taught me and my brothers not only hunting with a rifle but how to set traps. Sometimes, when the animal was caught it was still alive and we could keep it as a pet. I collected lots of wild pets such as birds and young boar.

Once, on an outing on his own, Dad caught a monkey in the trap. He shot her, but then found a baby clinging to the body. He brought it home and I kept the little monkey as my pet. I raised him for a year but he became very naughty. Once he nearly burned down our house, and he made a mess of our young mangos. So we decided to sell him to the merchant who visited my village.

My Dad was a good hunter, catching almost every kind of animal in the jungle, even big pythons and tigers. One night he shot a bear. He carried the body home like he was carrying a baby on his back. Everyone in the village came to have a look.

Chapter 6

Agony

Around this time my Mom stopped taking her traditional contraception and, seven months or so later, she fell pregnant again. Her pregnancy made Dad angry. He didn't want any more children.

The violence began again.

A man called Thongsavath arrived in the village. He was like a nomad without a home. He went around all over the district and stayed on if someone hired him for a job such as cutting wood, growing crops or putting up fences.

When he came to my village a family hired him to help them out on their farm. He met my sister Meuan and they started seeing each other regularly.

In Khmu culture if a man likes a woman he sends her a gift. The gift can be food such as fish, meat or vegetables. It has to come from his own efforts and not bought from someone else.

One morning, at breakfast, we were surprised by an uninvited visitor. A boy from the family where the itinerant labourer was staying had brought us some venison. He told us it was a gift from Thongsavath. My sister went red when we turned to her. She accepted the gift and the boy ran home.

After the meal my second sister Lae asked her who the man was. This was a conversation for the girls. They talked and laughed. Soon Dad called in my sister to talk to her. He told her not to see this guy again because nobody knew where he was from, where his village was, or who his family was. "Who knows, he might be a gangster!" Dad told her. But my sister didn't listen to him. A few days later she and Thongsavath met again.

At that Dad became very angry with her. He threatened to beat her up if she didn't stop seeing this guy. It still didn't stop them seeing each other.

After about a year Thongsavath came to talk to my parents to say he wanted my sister to be his wife. Dad didn't say much to him, but Mom said: "It's OK, he can have her." She was thinking that he might be able to help out the family with work because she was carrying her next child and Dad wasn't being as diligent as he had been.

Soon Thongsavath moved into our house and lived with us. They weren't married because he was poor. He didn't bring a dowry or anything to provide for my parents. Still, they had a small ceremony. And he was good. He worked a lot and was expert at hunting and fishing too.

Late one night, while we were all asleep Mom gave birth, alone, to my younger sister. We only woke up when we heard the sound of the new-born crying. Dad woke up too and helped her. I was very happy to have a younger sister. I was old enough to take care of her.

Later though, Dad became annoyed over having another baby. He started drinking a lot again, coming home drunk and messing up the house. He threw stuff around and smashed things. Meuan and her new husband couldn't endure the disorder so they decided to leave. They went to live with Ser and his new wife in their village, leaving us to cope with the violence on our own.

Running away

Living with our alcoholic father, so violent much of the time, was frightening. All he did was drink at home or come home drunk, kick the walls, smash up the house and beat my Mom if she confronted him. Sometimes he beat us as well, especially Lae when she tried to help Mom.

Many times me and Nid ran away from him. We were afraid he'd beat us up. Sometime we just didn't want to witness the horrible sight of him beating my Mom.

The worst part was being so powerless to stop him. We could do nothing, nothing at all.

Nid and I ran away to the farm several times. We made our way back home when we were hungry. But Dad hid the food and rice, just to punish us.

One of the more unpleasant aspects of our running away together was we got into fighting each other instead of sticking together.

Often we ran to my grandaunt Yahern's house

where we were fed and offered a bed for the night. We felt a lot safer than at home. Many times in the morning we quietly walked back to our house after spending the night there. When we arrived we would see Mom crying in the kitchen, still doing her chores. It felt like our father had given us life but he was destroying it at the same time. He gave me an instinct to run away.

Dad became more and more alcoholic and violent. Some of the time I looked after my little sister Noy. I took care of the chores at the same time. I wasn't able to join my Mom, brothers and sisters working at the farm.

When I had to be at home with my drunk father he slept throughout the day. Then he would wake up asking what was there to eat for him. Often he asked: 'Where is everyone?'

He ate whatever we had and then left to continue his drinking until the evening. He behaved like this for some time.

Many evenings when Mom and my siblings arrived home from working in the field my father would be lying in the middle of the floor, whining and angry. My Mom always tried her best to avoid him. That made him even more angry. Often they ended up fighting. The violence didn't always end up well, causing trouble for all of us. He smashed stuff and kicked the walls and furniture, beat up my mother, us sometimes. Only my sister Lae stayed in the house, every time, to help my mother. We were too young to stop him. Sometimes the fighting lasted until the next morning. The neighbours complained. They hated us for that as well.

One morning, as we all started our normal day, Mom was packing stuff for the farm. We had all dressed and were about to leave the house when Dad woke up, rose from the bed and started to insult her as soon as he saw us all ready to leave. He was angry because none of us wanted to be at home with him.

The argument began, followed by violence. Everything was ruined that morning. My Dad threw all the packing bags out of the house; rice and food was strewn all over the floor. Neighbours stood in front of their houses, staring.

Nid and I left the house for the farm by ourselves. We brought nothing with us. There was no food or rice left.

It took us nearly an hour to walk slowly to the farm that morning. It was cold and painful. At the same time we were confused with all that was happening to the family. Why couldn't we just have normal lives and a normal family like everyone else?

When we reached the farm we were tired and hungry. We rested for a short while in the hut, then we went to find some cucumbers to satisfy our hunger. They were young and green so we didn't pick many.

We rested a bit more. When we got hungrier we started to trudge back home. On the way we stopped at the stream to catch crabs and snails.

We arrived home in mid-afternoon, expecting at least some rice. But there was none. The house was empty. I ran to my grandaunt's house expecting to see Mom or my sister but none of them was there. Before we turned back for home again I begged for some rice and chili. When we got back, we cooked crabs and snails for our first meal of the day. Later we found out Mom and Lae had gone out to pick bamboo shoots and wild vegetables. Noy and Sone were out playing somewhere. Dad was drinking at someone else's house, as usual. Nobody cared.

I tried my best to be grown up and work my way out of the situation, but I still had my childlike instincts, wanting to play when I saw other children enjoying themselves. I didn't have much fun. Still, I was happy enough to watch other kids playing.

While I was searching for Noy I encountered quite unpleasant, random older women who demanded to know what was wrong with my family. Why were we such trouble, making noise to disturb everyone nearby? Their questions bothered me. It wasn't fair to question me instead of Dad. I wanted to tell them: "Go ask my father!"

Soon I found my little sister. She was stealing someone else's green tamarind. I joined in. As we tried to bring some of the tamarind down, using a bamboo stick, the owner caught us in the act. She was angry and yelled at us, trying to shame us.

I know stealing is bad but it was just a tamarind and not a lot of it. I had the feeling that she was angry because it was us. She would have reacted differently if it had been someone else.

A scandalous affair

With Dad's alcoholism getting worse than ever, he did something that no-one in the village had ever done. He had an affair with someone else's wife. Despite it being such a small village they were seeing each other for quite a while before they were caught by her husband.

The news spread all over the village as soon as they were caught. The villagers looked on us even more differently.

A trial in the village was quickly organised. Mom and Dad, the woman with whom he had an affair and her husband were all called in. The woman's husband sued my father and he was fined K300,000[3] and a cow. That amount, around $40 now, was a lot in a village at that time.

Mom ended up paying all the fine for Dad. She sold her last gold necklace, one her mother had given to her as a child before the war. She had to sell a cow as well to reach the amount the husband had been adjudged.

Dad, instead of apologising for what he had done and thanking Mom for helping him out, became very angry when she confronted him at home after the trial. He became very violent. We all ran to Yahern's to hide. Only my sister Lae stayed there to help Mom. Lae was beaten by her father as well in the end. It was almost midnight when my brothers and I came back to the house to sleep. Mom cried all night as my baby sister slept. I slept next to her. Lae spent the rest of the night at Yahern's house to hide from Dad.

---

[3] The Lao unit of currency is the kip. In 2022 the exchange rate was roughly K12,000 to the US dollar.

Early next morning she came home quietly, cooked some rice and left for the farm alone. Me, Mom with baby Noy, and my two brothers went after her. I could see the bruises on my mother's face. Her mouth was cut.

The day was better for not having Dad around us. It was peaceful and loving. No sounds of argument. Nothing. Mom was very quiet. Nid and I built ourselves a little hut and caught grasshoppers to eat. We came home very late. When we arrived we didn't see my father in the house.

We finally had a quiet sleep. It was the best!

Catching pangolins

After the scandal surrounding my father villagers started to keep their distance. Children looked askance at us, as if we'd done something to them. People gossiped. My father tried to stay away as much as he could. He might have been ashamed of what he had done and didn't want to hear people talk about it. He spent most of his time working at the farm, then went out hunting animals by night. Mom cooked for him. She couldn't help with hard work given her young child.

Lae and Sone helped a lot. As they grew older they had become very diligent, especially Lae. Sometimes she complained that my parents' farm was too small. There wasn't enough work, she said!

Mom and the others travelled back and forth between the farm and village whereas Dad stayed there for long stretches. But sometimes we also spent days and nights there without coming back. It was like our second home. It was tiring to walk back and forth over such a long distance.

As time passed my family returned to normal. We found some peace. No more violence. But people in the village still looked at us differently. We ignored them and only came to the village once in a while.

Everyone was growing up and working hard. I helped my parents by taking care of Noy, bringing them water during the day while they worked. Sometimes I prepared vegetables and called my sister to come and cook for lunch. My Mom would come to the hut every hour to feed Noy.

Sometimes Sone and Nid, around 12 and 10 years old at the time, went hunting on their own. They set traps and sometimes caught birds, squirrels and field rats. Even Lae learned how to fish. I was around six years old. In the countryside that age is when the parents start to train their children to work and how to survive alone in the forest. People didn't talk about school. Parents taught their children how to farm, hunt and raise livestock. Kids in the village grew up and got married at a young age and quickly established their own families. No one knew a life outside this.

My father told us many times: "You don't have to go anywhere else!" All he wanted was to let us inherit whatever he had worked on. He wanted us to become farmers and be good hunters like himself. None of the older people knew what it was like to live in a big town. None of them had ever been to a big town or seen a car.

They said: "Don't dream of something else apart from becoming farmers." Anything other than that would be impossible for forest people like us, they said.

Harvest season came at the end of November. The weather became colder and villagers finished gathering in their rice and other crops. My family did the same and we had to come back to the village because no more work was left to do.

It was four months before the farming season started again so as well as hunting Dad and some of his friends went looking for pangolins. Merchants from the town used to come looking for them and used to offer a high price. But the animals had to be caught alive. Otherwise the merchants wouldn't buy. Some people were lucky, catching three or four and selling them for a good price. One time Dad caught two and sold them for K400,000 (around $45). That was a lot. My parents were able to buy clothes for all of us. We all got a pair of pants and a shirt. None of the children wore shoes then. I got my first pair when I was nine.

Pangolins are tricky animals because they can hide themselves inside a hole or a cave and even on top of big trees. And it's hard to catch them during the day because they can run very fast. Many hunters lose their catch when they try to pull a pangolin out of a hole because their sharp, strong nails make it so hard to drag them out. Spotting and catching them in the trees is the most difficult because they run right to the topmost branches where we can't reach. Often hunters have no choice but to shoot them and, of course, they can't sell dead pangolins but at least they have the meat to feed their families.

My Dad and I went catching pangolins together sometimes. It wasn't easy. We had to go deep into a cave and use a torch to spot them, where the bats also lived. They could run very fast. But sometimes we would catch up and the moment we touched them they shrunk up into a ball and stopped moving. That's when we grabbed them.

My Dad earned quite a lot of money from pangolins. It was the richest period we ever had.

Lightning strikes

One night Dad went hunting by himself. It was raining heavily. So, instead of coming home he decided to spend the night in a small cave. A bolt of lightning struck. Dad fell unconscious. He woke up and his nose was bleeding.

When he came home his skin was pale. He looked exhausted. He washed himself and went to bed. We didn't know what had happened. We thought he might just be tired. He told us nothing.

In the afternoon he woke up. His nose was still bleeding. I was very afraid and worried for him. My Mom gave him traditional medicine. He rested again. When he woke up we had dinner together. He was unusually quiet. It wasn't farming season so he was able to rest at home. Soon he improved and started to work again. But the nose bleed recurred every few days.

Eventually, he got back to working and hunting

like he normally did. And about six months later my Mom gave birth to our youngest sister, Pone.

Ten days after the birth my parents gave little Pone away to a couple in the village who had no children. Soon she died. No-one knew why.

Then Dad's symptoms started to recur more strongly. He had a headache and nose bleed almost every day. Finally, while I was out hunting, he told my Mom what had happened that night in the small cave.

She talked to a shaman and he told her that we had to perform a ritual. He said it was bad luck and we would have to sacrifice a duck. She did what she was told and organised a Baci ceremony to bring Dad luck and good health.

Me and my brothers replaced our father, fishing and hunting with traps. We couldn't provide much for our family but it was enough some of the time. Dad was very proud of us.

We never talked about my oldest sister Meuan who had left to live with my grandfather again. She never came to visit us.

Big town debut

As Dad's illness worsened we realised we had to look for another way to cure him. After using traditional medicine many times and employing shamans to perform rituals his symptoms had not improved at all.

With all the money we had left from selling pangolins we decided to go to the town of Luang

Prabang to have my father treated at the hospital there. It was going to be my first time in a town so I was very excited. I was so curious to know what the town – and a car – would look like.

I woke up especially early. As soon as I heard my Mom wake up to cook sticky rice I jumped off the bed, cleaned my face, brushed my teeth and put on my new clothes. But it was still dark. So I sat there waiting expectantly for the new day to start.

Finally Mom finished cooking. She made me a special sticky rice cake. I gobbled it, finished the rest of my breakfast, helped her pack and went down to feed the chickens. I was so excited.

My siblings woke up and they were jealous, especially Nid when he saw me all prepared in my new clothes. Only me and Noy were going, along with Mom and Dad. Soon I would be seeing the Nam Ou, one of the biggest rivers in Laos, as well as the town. People in the village spoke of the many mysteries of the river, some saying huge snakes that ate people swam in it and some saying the fish could be as big as cows.

Down by the riverbank we had to wait for a boat to pass so we could hop on. It seemed like it would never arrive. I was so impatient. 'When is it coming, when is it coming?' I pestered my Mom.

Finally a long-boat arrived and we hopped on. My older siblings lined up wistfully at the pier looking at us as our boat pulled away. My Dad told them all to behave themselves while we were away. I had a big smile on my face.

After about an hour we came to a high bridge crossing the river. Suddenly, I saw a truck passing over. My heart thumped. It was the first time I had seen either the main road or even a vehicle.

The boat pulled up by the bridge and we hopped out. It was around noon so we cooked up our meal by the side of the road, waiting for an open truck to come. An hour later a truck finally did arrive, so we clambered in and my Dad paid what the driver asked.

As soon as the truck started to move I felt faint. The feeling was so weird. After about 10 minutes me and my Mom threw up from carsickness. It was a horrible feeling. Already I so regretted coming along. "I could just have stayed home and gone setting bird traps," I thought to myself. Dad laughed at both of us getting sick. The journey seemed to take forever and I hated every bit of it.

After about two hours Dad pointed with his finger. When I turned around I saw a river, wide and filthy. It was the great Nam Ou, and no sign of a giant snake.

We arrived at Luang Prabang bus station late. There I was mesmerised by all the little tuk-tuks, the three-wheeled motorbike taxis with roofs. We clambered into one and when the driver asked where we were going Dad tried to tell him that we were heading for the hospital. The driver didn't get it at first because of Dad's stumbling attempt at speaking Lao. None of us spoke the national language properly. Us forest people may as well have been in a foreign country. The guy was kind and patient though, listening carefully to what Dad was trying to explain.

Finally he understood and headed off for the

hospital. It was midnight by the time we reached it, 13 hours after setting off, but this time the doctor couldn't understand what Dad was saying. She called in a Khmu man to talk to him. He told us to wait till tomorrow, showed us a room and we settled down there for the night.

I barely slept in the strange environment. "This is why people don't leave their village — life in a different place is tough," I thought to myself.

A dirty 'waterfall'

I woke up to the noise of trucks and motorbikes out on the street and the sound of people yelling. It was all so unfamiliar, so different. No birds sang, no smell of a fresh morning breeze. People ran around, back and forth, in and out of the dirty old hospital building. A boy crying sounded different from what I'd heard in the village.

Merchants carrying baskets flocked in to sell their food. Me and my Mom stood there watching all this strangeness for a while before she silently went inside to wake up Dad and my sister. I could tell she hated it just as much as me.

Outside the building in the car park Mom set a fire to cook our sticky rice using the dry sticks she had carried on her back. It's what Khmu do when they're on the move. We bring sticky rice, a cooking pot and firewood everywhere we go, especially if we're staying some place for a while. With some money saved to exchange for food we use the fire to make it feel more like home, our possessions nothing more than the impromptu hearth of sticks and branches, a pot for sticky rice and stew, and us gathered round on our haunches, comfortable with ourselves.

Dad brought Noy and joined us around the stove. We watched other kids play while their parents were busy preparing their breakfast. Soon afterwards the Khmu man called Dad inside and Mom followed him in, leaving me and little Noy to take care of the rice. They came back soon after, once Dad had been diagnosed and they had given him some medication. We had our breakfast, Dad took his pills and we went back inside where Dad was given a bed for his stay. The doctor came in to give him an injection. I had never seen that before. The sharp needle looked very scary and painful.

Soon Noy and I went outside to explore. We stood against the low white wall, watching bicycles and trucks pass by on the street. The children had toys and they were walking along a paved road. They wore nice clothes and had shoes on their feet. We watched contentedly and smiled.

Days passed in the town and seemed very long. We became very homesick. I missed my brothers and sisters so much. At one point I was straying around the hospital grounds on my own, exploring, when I spotted water running out of a concrete hole. I knew a waterfall when I saw one. It was a steady stream so I went to find a bottle, filled it and was washing my hands when Mom suddenly arrived. "Get away from that dirty water!" she yelled. She dragged me into the building, shoved my hands under a tap and washed them vigorously.

I had no idea the waterfall was just an outlet pipe and the water was sewage. In the village, when I saw water come from a rock or a tree it was always clean and you could drink it. Not around here.

Six days passed but to me it felt more like a month. Finally my father improved and we decided to go home. Before we went to the bus station we paid a visit to the market. I spied so many toys. My Dad bought himself a pair of trousers and some crackers for my siblings. My sister cried for a shirt, and was given one. I saw a cute little teddy bear and grabbed it, thinking Dad would buy it for me. He told me to put it back. I nearly cried. Mom suggested that, instead of the teddy, I collect elastic bands off the floor. By the time we left the market I had a pile of them so I could knot them in a row and play jumping rope.

The journey home was just as bad as when we came. Me and my Mom became so sick again. So as soon as our boat pulled up to the pier by our village I felt like I was back in heaven. My brothers and sisters were standing on the rock waiting for us with their big smiles. Lae took Noy in her arms and everyone admired her new shirt. We all walked home together. They told us that they had run to the pier every time they heard the sound of a boat coming, hoping to see us arrive.

Dad's illness returns

A month after we came back from hospital Dad fell very ill. The hospital hadn't treated him properly at all. We're not sure if they knew what was wrong. They had given him some tablets but they didn't help.

Soon the farming season started and my Mom, sister and brothers worked without him. My Dad stayed at home with me and my little sister. I was around seven years old by then so I was old enough to look after my sister and take care of the chores. Every day my Mom woke up early, cooked and prepared for their trip to the field. Sometimes she cooked and took the food with them, leaving some for us. But sometimes I had to cook myself and boil the water for Dad. He usually woke up very late. Me and my little sister would have our breakfast, and sometimes we would go for a short walk. Other times though we had to stay in the house because our father needed help.

As the sickness got worse my father lost his voice. We couldn't hear him at all when he spoke from any distance. Often he had to shout, which made him more stressed. Often he just hit the floor with a piece of wood when he needed something. He had become tired of shouting.

One afternoon while he was having a nap, we heard a loud bang on the roof. It's made of galvanised steel so it was really loud. A boy who had got annoyed with my brother Sone had thrown a big stone onto the roof. He couldn't hit Sone so he messed about with our house instead.

Waking up startled, Dad was very angry. He hit the window with his stick very hard. The boy was frightened so he screamed and ran off to his house. Later his father, the village chief, came and got very angry at Dad. He shouted and insulted him. His shouting stirred the neighbours to come and watch what was happening. And, of course, those people despised us for that as well.

My Dad didn't say anything at the time but when Sone came back home he beat him up for causing the trouble. Poor Sone was thrown out of the house and broke his ankle. And to prevent this from happening again Dad also beat me and Nid.

But that was the last time Dad was violent.

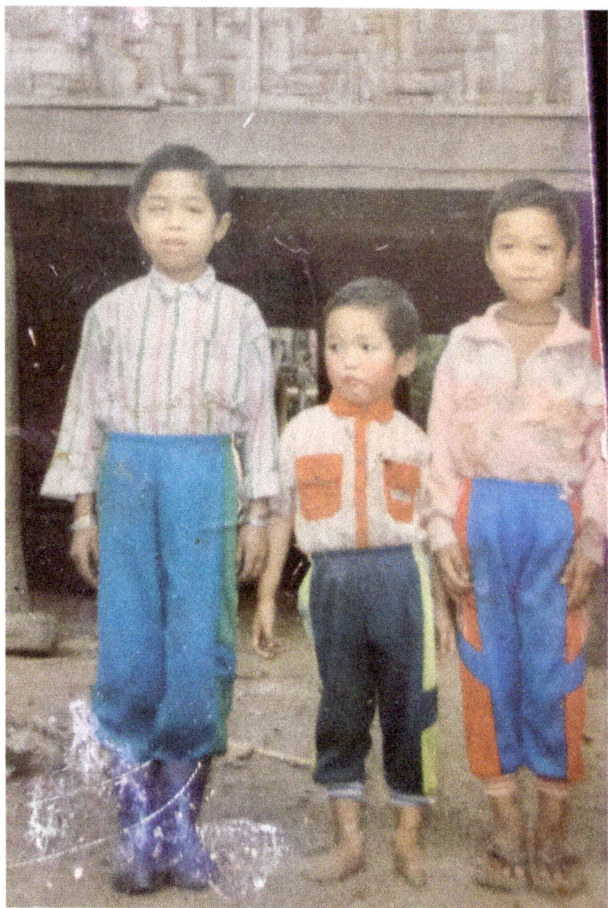

Sone, Nat and Nid

Chapter 7

The end

About eight months passed. Dad's illness reached its last stage. He could no longer talk or walk. He spent most of his time in bed. Every few hours his nose bled. Noy and Sone didn't want to get close to him, especially when his nose was bleeding. They were scared of him. He was so skinny and pale. We didn't recognise his face anymore.

We were so hungry, nearly starving, yet others in the village kept on bullying us, showing nothing but a total lack of respect even as we suffered.

Often me and little Noy had to go into the forest to look for bamboo shoots and wild potatoes for a meal. We had no rice left. My Mom, Lae and Sone went to work for other families, putting up fences, carrying rice from their farms to the village or clearing grass in return for some rice or any other scraps to eat.

Sometimes we three brothers went hunting on our own. We set lots of traps and caught some birds, but mostly small animals like field rats and mice. We kept no pet now because we needed any food for ourselves.

One morning all the food was gone. There was nothing left. I was so hungry. I cried and cried. In the late afternoon I decided to go to Yahern and beg her for help. She gave me a bit of rice and a few chilis. I came home and ate that. I gave some to Dad.

One day, a Vietnamese couple from Vientiane Capital came to my village looking for boys and girls to work in a garment factory in the city. Lae was around 17 at the time. Two girls and a boy offered to go along with them. One of them was Lae. Someone had to do something to provide for the family. We organised a little Baci ceremony for her to wish her luck. And they left the next morning. I was very sad. We were all very sad.

We survived mainly with the help of Phou's son who gave us some corn and rice from time to time. Sometimes Yahern gave me and Noy some food. We often shared it with Dad. My Mom and two brothers ate when they were out working for someone else. They often got fed during the day working for those people.

One day Mom and Sone worked hard for a family and at the end of the day they gave us quite a bit of rice. It was more than we expected so we were happy. But we hadn't realised that there were just husks at the bottom of the bag to make it look more. We felt so hurt.

About a month after the three young people went off to the factory in Vientiane, the boy and girl who went with Lae returned. They said it was too difficult. They hadn't been able to get enough sleep, and the owner didn't feed them properly. Lae didn't come but along with them she sent us K60,000 (about $7). The boy and girl handed over only K40,000 though. Still, we had enough to buy rice for two weeks. We added wild potatoes to the rice so we could stretch out our supplies.

It was very cold, late November. Village had finished their harvesting. It was time for a break, time to stay at home with families. The men went out hunting, children set fires at home and gathered around, cooking sweet potatoes and telling ghost stories.

Life was so lonely for me. Often I sat on the balcony and watched the other kids playing. But me and my little sister had to take turns to look after our father while the other one was out foraging for food or going to fetch water.

One night, around the end of November, as my Mom was about to fall sleep, the sound of a rock wall collapsing came from a cave near the village. A bad sign. A rock collapsing meant someone in the village would die sooner or later.

Dad, as hard as it was for him to talk, tried to tell my Mom to call our souls back home. People believe that their souls will be taken away by the spirits if a rock collapses. I was very scared. I didn't feel right. Our father was so sick.

I think Dad knew that he was about to die. After my Mom called our souls back, he said: "I'm afraid that I won't get to see Lae again."

My Mom and I didn't sleep at all.

Next morning Mom decided to stay home. My

two brothers went out to set their traps. Mom boiled some water and made us some rice cake. We ate our breakfast. Then she went to the bedroom to wake Dad up, wash his face and give him his breakfast. But he wasn't breathing.

He was dead.

I heard my Mom cry from inside the bedroom. I knew what had happened. She told me to go and fetch Phou's son. I ran there and told him the news. He came over and cried.

My brothers came home, laden with birds and field rats. They knew Dad had died. Someone had told them before they reached the village.

The funeral was so quiet and small. Only Phou's family and his aunt Yahern, along with a few people who didn't hate us, came along.

The body was kept out for only one night. They buried Dad the next morning.

It was raining that day. I didn't go to the graveyard for the ceremony. Only Nid went along with a few others to bury Dad. We hired a man, along with his nephew, to help carry his coffin. And since we didn't have the money to pay the man my Mom and brother had to compensate him by working on his farm for three days.

Usually after a funeral people come and stay with the family so they don't become fearful during the night. But nobody came, except Phou's son. He stayed with us for a few nights.

My Mom said that two days after Dad's passing she heard his spirit coming home around midnight. The sound was very like him. She was very frightened.

Sad news

Traditionally, a family doesn't leave the village for seven days after someone dies. In this seven-day period my Mom prepared food in banana leaves and went with incense sticks to the cemetery as an offering to my father's spirit. My older brothers often went with her, and sometimes I accompanied them.

Each time when we reached the cemetery we had to sit down and place the banana leaves, full of food, on the ground. Then we would light the incense and my Mom would call my father's name. This was to let him know that we were bringing him food and from now on he shouldn't bother us because we were no longer connected.

"You belong to your world and we belong to ours. We are no longer family," she called out to him.

This was to let the spirit know that he was no longer a part of our lives. Otherwise, he would keep coming back and never find his way to where he now belonged.

I believe Dad must have been reunited with his parents and brother somewhere.

Animists tell stories about the spirit kingdom, a world different from ours, a world where people live for eternity. It's a world where people are reunited with their loved ones. It's full of happiness, magical. It's very close to our own world, but we just can't see them. Just like they can't see us.

Every time I visited the cemetery I was

frightened because of the belief that the spirit would come and eat the food immediately after we walked away. We were not supposed to look back. Otherwise we would see the spirit and it would take our souls away.

We always had to go in the evening. We had to walk through the thick forest there and back, just as darkness was about to fall. I couldn't decide between how scared I was and how much I missed my father. It felt about fifty-fifty.

We were all sad immediately afterwards, but we had been aware that this time would come sooner or later. He'd been sick for nearly two years. What made it most sad was that Lae wasn't with us and we had no way to let her know because she lived so far away.

Seven days after my father's passing we were again able to leave the village. Someone had to deliver the news to my other sister, Meuan. So on the morning of the eighth day, I headed out early, down towards the river. I was around eight years old. I had my little bag with me, with some extra clothing and some rice to eat along the way.

I quietly walked down to the river and waited there for grandaunt Yahern. When she arrived I had to take off my clothes because the river was deep. Even up on my tiptoes the water lapped above my chin. It was so cold. But we reached the other side.

We walked along a misty road. A cold breeze blew. Winter flowers smelt fresh. The song of the morning birds reminded me of times when I had gone out hunting with my father, when our family had walked to the farm as one. Just memories now.

I was so confused. I walked very quickly, ahead of my grandaunt. I cried quietly.

I missed my Dad, I missed my sister, I missed everything. It was only the second time I had left my family, but this time was different from last. No excitement, only sadness. I was afraid my grandfather's new wife wouldn't like me.

We walked for more than nine hours, barefoot. We walked up and down mountains, crossed streams and stopped for rest at deserted farm huts. We picked wild flowers.

But when we got to my grandfather's village Meuan wasn't there. She and her husband were working at the farm.

Only my grandfather and his new wife were at home. It felt so strange to be in this new village with someone I called "grandpa", who had left us when we needed him the most.

They offered us some lunch and, while we were eating, his sister Yahern told him about Dad's passing. All he said was: "That is his karma. He deserved it." His words made me angry. I had lost my Dad. Everyone in the family was desperate. And all he could do was dig up the past against a dead person for his own satisfaction.

My step-grandmother was a nice lady. She asked me throughout the day if I needed more banana or sugar cane. She asked me many questions about my family and other things. Her kindness warmed me.

My sister and her husband arrived home from the farm in the evening. I told her the news and she cried. She asked about everyone. I told her that Lae had been gone for several months and she still didn't know about our Dad's passing.

I stayed at my grandfather's village for four days. I really missed my Mom and my siblings but I was happy to get to see my sister and brother-in-law again after such a long time. My grandfather didn't talk to me that much. I think he still got angry over what my father had done to him, how he had thrown him and his wife out of his own home. He had a step-grandson of whom he was really fond. Every time he spoke to me he brought up the subject of his step-grandson, making him sound so much cooler. I didn't like listening to that.

On the fourth day, before I headed back, Meuan asked me to come with her to her farm. There she filled a big bag with sticky rice and bananas and handed it to me. She didn't want my grandfather to see it. I don't know why. Maybe he wouldn't be happy if he knew my sister was giving me food.

Yahern and I left early. We walked back along the same pathway through the forest. I carried a big load on my head. It was so heavy I slipped and fell on my butt many times. The path was often steep, up and down so many mountains.

We got home in the early evening. My Mom and siblings were happy to have me back.

Village bullies

Even after my father died the bullying and hatefulness remained a big problem for my family. It came mostly from the children and elderly people.

The legacy of my father was a gift from a tormented time. People looked at us as no more than objects towards which they could direct whatever ill feeling they felt.

Not long after Dad died our family contracted an illness, some kind of skin disease that caused a rash and swelling under the skin. It may have been caused by the unclean environment where we lived, or some food we had eaten. Most of the villagers thought it was contagious. They were disgusted and made that clear. No one in the village wanted to come close to us. They used the skin condition to bully us. We had become outcasts, the lepers of our village.

One evening when Nid and I went to collect grasshoppers for supper a girl called at us from behind with a bullying word that related to our disease. She ran away and came back, repeating it over and over again. I couldn't bear to hear her hateful word, so I ran after her and punched her on the back. She ran home crying to her parents. Her Mom came and beat me up. My Mom was angry that the woman did that to me so she approached her and demanded: "Why did she do that? It's a thing between the kids."

They argued loudly. The whole village came to watch. No one stood up for us. The woman who beat me up was a relative of the village chief. He came along and directed his anger at Mom. He called us a disgrace to everyone. He told us to leave the village. He said he would pay the cost of going wherever we wanted to go. When Mom asked him if he would provide us with the cost of building a home in the new place as well, he just got more angry.

That long, horrible night never seemed to end.

Before Lae left to work in a garment factory in Vientiane Capital the whole community had accused her of being a prostitute. We had no place to hide our faces. Whoever wanted to let their anger out would pick on us. "Shame on you for having a sister being a prostitute," they would spit with disgust.

Our problems were no longer ours as a family, this had become Lae's own problem. That was partly why she had left for the capital with the two other girls. But the nastiness didn't stop. One time when she came to visit, the accusers talked loudly about her behind her back as she walked through the village. They gossiped right in front of her, and us. We tried to ignore them as much as we could because responding to them would have done nothing but cause more trouble. One time Lae became so angry because of the bullying she told Mom that she would never come back to the village.

Yet, when she brought a sewing machine, one of the first such machines in my home town, a lot of people flocked to our house to get Lae to mend their clothes and tailor their skirts. She didn't charge them any money. All she wanted, and us, was some respect and to be treated like everyone else.

Elderly people in particular were prejudiced against us. Every time I walked along the street they would call me in and ask me things like what would I eat later. "Who will provide for you guys now, since your father is dead?" "Where did you get the rice?" They never offered any.

It made me sick in my stomach that these people were so curious to know what was going on in my family. We couldn't have peace. The best way to stay out of their hatefulness was to go and spend as much time as we could at the farm.

One time when water buffalos ate the rice and crops in our farm we went and talked to the owners. Instead of apologising and compensating us for any loss they became angry instead and threatened to kick out of the village. Given our status, they felt able to do that.

Machete attack

It was a while since my father had not been with us. We were slowly getting used to living without him.

We three brothers, as well as Mom, became the main source of food for the family. Well, I was small so I didn't do that much apart from taking care of chores and setting traps to catch birds and field rats. Sometimes little Noy came along. Sone went hunting, like Dad. Nid mostly helped Mom in the field. We also raised chickens. The eggs provided us with food from time to time. Two eggs made a meal for the whole family. We made egg soup with vegetables and herbs.

Mom would wake up early in the morning to cook rice and feed the chickens then we would prepare for our trip to the farm.

Life slowly became a little easier because we no

longer had to stay at home to take care of our sick father. We worked from early morning and came back home late in the evening, almost every day, just to survive.

Lae came to visit us every once in awhile. She brought us gifts from the city such as crackers, and clothing that she had sewn herself.

One day we were all at home because it was our family's holiday (the anniversary of my father's passing).

While I was helping my Mom to husk rice two brothers from our neighbour's house started fighting. The younger one had a big rusty machete. He chased his big brother but he couldn't catch him. Seeing me sitting there he decided his chance had come. He slashed at my head with his rusty blade. With little warning, I found myself lying on the ground, soaked in blood that spurted from my head and face.

My Mom ran to me, grabbed the machete from the boy, and threw it away. Then, lifting me in her arms, she ran down to the bush beyond the village and scrabbled for a plant called Jidkeo. Its leaves can stanch bleeding. She chewed some of the leaves before pressing the wad to the gash in my head. Soon the bleeding stopped and she carried me home.

I developed a high fever later that day. The boy's parents came over and apologised for what their son had done. They gave us a chicken to sacrifice for a Baci ceremony for me. Soon my head became infected. It was very painful. My Mom kept putting traditional herbs on the wound and covering it up with fabric. It took a month and I only slowly got better.

Lae came to visit us and brought me some nice shoes. It was the first time I had my own.

The family all loved me, especially my sister Lae. Every time she came home she brought a gift for me, even when she didn't have one for everyone else.

In some ways I inherited my father's looks. Tall and slim, with pale skin. These features reminded my family of our father. Everyone in the village said so. Many times I was walking along and people mentioned to me: "You really have your father's likeness."

A dreadful time had passed. Soon I got back to my normal eight-year-old's work.

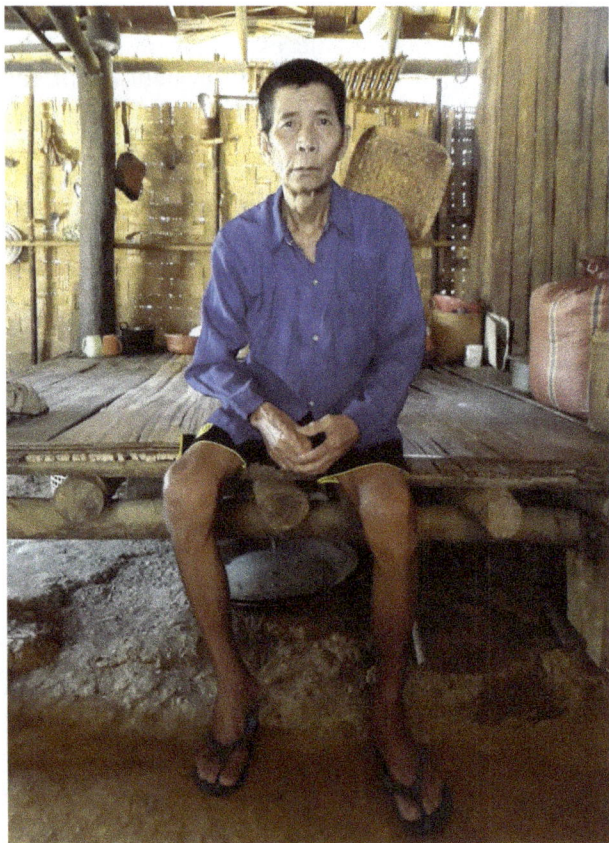

Grandpa

Chapter 8

Surviving

About two months after Dad died, just after harvest, the December weather turned cold, but it was still a busy time with preparation for Khmu New Year. The villagers were excited in anticipation of the festival, especially the children and teenagers. They sold or exchanged some of their rice harvest for new clothes from passing merchants.

Those who didn't have much rice, such as us, tried to make some money by harvesting wild date seeds instead. Dates mostly grow in the thick jungle, especially near streams where the temperature drops. The crop is worth quite a bit of money, especially for white seeds. City people use them in desserts and they are also sold to China. But, in order to harvest the dates, villagers have to spend at least a few days and nights in the jungle to gather enough to sell. My family was one of those used to doing that.

My Mom, Sone, me and Noy woke up early one

cold morning and packed whatever we needed for several nights in the forest. Nid didn't join us because we needed someone to take care of the house.

We packed our cooking pot with sticky rice, salt, chili and MSG and tied it with a rope. Also bowls, spoons, matches, machetes, a big knife and a bucket as well as big nylon bags for the seeds themselves. And a huge pot for boiling the dates. Also warm clothes. Then we started walking. It took us until noon, around six hours, to reach a place where we thought we might find some date trees. First we found a bamboo stand, cut plenty of long branches and put together a cosy bamboo hut. It took us several hours to finish the building work.

I made a fire and cooked the rice while my Mom and Sone went off to find something to cook for dinner. Noy was sitting quietly beside the stove. It was really cold and it would get dark pretty quickly.

After a while we became scared because Mom and Sone hadn't come back yet. We kept adding firewood to the fire, to make it much bigger. The fire scares the animals away, and the spirits.

Soon though Mom and Sone appeared. They had caught some crabs and banana flowers which we cooked for our dinner. And then we went to sleep. It was really, really cold throughout the night. I didn't sleep well and neither did my Mom. She kept waking up to add more firewood because of the biting cold.

Next morning, after breakfast, we started to explore the area to see if we could find some dates. Soon we found a tree, then another and another.

And they were full of dates ready for harvesting. Sone was a good climber, so he shinnied up like a monkey, a big knife tied with a piece of string to his back. Then he hacked off the dates at the top, dropped them to the ground where we collected them, put them into the bags and carried them back to our little camp.

We repeated this over and over until we had enough.

But extracting the seeds isn't easy. First we had to boil the fruit for at least an hour. Then we cut the heads and pressed the fruit to push the seeds out. The hardest part was when we cut the fruit to boil it. Each piece of fruit is very itchy inside and handling is uncomfortable.

Because the fruit is big and the seeds are very small it took us three days and nights, working non-stop. The cutting and pressing took a lot of time. From three pots of dates we only got half a pot of seeds. So we had to amass fruit for at least 20 pots just for our one big bag of seeds. And we had to get back home in time to sell the seeds. Otherwise they would have turned grey and nobody would buy them.

After four days and three nights in the forest we finally had nearly two big bags of seeds. They were very heavy.

My Mom carried one full bag, my brother took more than half of the second, and I brought the rest as well our personal belongings and the big pot. Finally, four-year-old Noy brought up the rear with her small bag for our clothes. Then we walked barefoot all the way home.

Next morning we carried our seeds down to the pier and the merchants soon arrived in their boats. They weighed our bags, paid us fairly and we earned enough money for our new year celebration. As well as that we bought some beef, and Mom bought us new trousers and a pair of flip-flops for herself.

It was a fun, although difficult, way of making money.

Grass money

In mid-February, about four months after my father died, the new farming season was in sight. Villagers brought their machetes, axes and big knives to the blacksmith's house so he could work on them. Some people paid in money, while others paid with rice or other crops to have their blades sharpened. My Mom brought some of our rice. But we didn't have enough, or any possibly, so she and Sone compensated by helping out with the work. They did did this by pressing on the blacksmith's elbow as he worked the sharpener.

The long grass used for brooms, also called Thysanolaena, was also blooming. We knew that merchants from the village nearby would come to our settlement, as they did each year, to buy the harvest as material for their brooms.

One morning we all woke up early. It was the coldest time of year so we made sticky rice cakes and kept ourselves warm by gathering around the fire. But the sky, bathed in mist and fog, was shrouded in grey until almost noon. When the sun finally started to break through people started to put their rice outside to dry. They would soon separate the grains with their homemade husking machines.

For older children it was time to pack their bags and head out from the village to harvest the long grass. I sat on the steps of our house watching them carry their bags down to the river to cross to the other side. Noy came out to join me with a big rice cake in her hands.

We had been sitting there for a while, watching the activity but too young to join in, when my Mom asked us if we could go harvest the grass ourselves as well. We could sell it to the merchants coming to our village tomorrow. "We have a small knife and a little bag that you can use for now, and the rest of the knives we can take to the blacksmith," she said.

A little later she prepared and packed us some rice and chili paste for the trip. She brought it outside and, once my sister had finished her rice cake, we headed for the river. As we waded in, I gripped the bag in my left hand, and Noy's arm in my right. She was only four years old. The water was so cold. It was dry season so it wasn't too deep but the current was still strong. We pushed across, scrambled out on the other side and quickly dressed again and started walking.

Along the way we met a few men carrying big prey back to the village. They were returning from an overnight hunt. I was stung with the reminder of my father. Suddenly I missed him, and our time out hunting together.

We kept on walking for a while until we came to a young part of the forest, clinging to a steep slope. We hauled ourselves up, which took quite some time. Plenty of Thysanolaena grass was growing there. I started to cut and clear a space to put our bag down. Then we started to slice through the grass. I left the cuttings in little piles along the way and continued on until we had enough. Then we turned round and collected the bundles all the way back to where we had started, like Hansel and Gretel collecting breadcrumbs.

We cut quite a lot. I chopped some string from a jungle vine to make handles for the grass. Noy carried the bag as well as some of the grass. Then we headed home, stopping along the way to enjoy our lunch. When we reached the river, I asked her to wait for me while I first took everything to the other side. Then I waded back to retrieve her. We spent some time swimming, ridding ourselves of the itch from the grass's flowers. Then we carried our load home.

To be sold, the grass had to be dried and all of its flowers cleaned out. Otherwise it would be very itchy. The drying took most of the next day, with the grass laid out in the sunlight. Then we cleaned out the flowers. Finally we tidied the grass up into neat bundles and our products were ready to sell. It was dark before we finished.

Next morning all the children, including Noy and I, took our grass down to the pier. Soon the merchants arrived in their boats. They weighed our grass and gave us some money. It was K1,500, about 15 pence, my first earnings. We handed the takings over to Mom who used it to buy salt and MSG. She had K300 left, so she gave it to me to pay a neighbour to join others and watch their television. For my three pence I got to watch a Lao comedy show, and some traditional singing on the black and white set. I loved it.

Slash and burn

The end of March brings the beginning of the farming season itself. Villagers clear away bush and forest to start their farms, a new patch each year. It is a very hot time of the year so farmers leave the cuttings they've cleared until everything is properly dried. Then, about a month later, they burn their fields.

Setting fire to a field can be dangerous. Sone and I nearly burned ourselves to a crisp once. Because the leaves are bone dry they catch fire very quickly. He began at one side of the cleared area and I started at the other. Moving inwards, he started to light one spot, then another, while I did the same from my side.

Suddenly, we found ourselves caught at the centre of a huge conflagration. Smoke was everywhere. We panicked. We couldn't find a way out. Sone grabbed my hand and dragged me straight into dense, white smoke. He knew that when the smoke was white the flames would not have started to shoot up just yet. We pushed on through smoke and branches and, somehow, we landed ourselves on the far side of the flames. We ran to the stream nearby and jumped in to protect ourselves from the heat.

About two hours later we walked up and inspected the area to see if some parts hadn't burned properly yet. It was all OK and after another half an hour we decided to return home. My Mom was worried when we got back because we had been away such a long time.

Villagers usually burn their new fields by early evening before returning home as the light fades. Next morning they go back to rummage around for any dead animals that might have been left behind from the burning and that provide some fresh meat.

Noy and I woke early next morning. We walked across the river and on for another 30 minutes until we reached our new farmland. Along the way we saw people exploring their own plots searching for dead animals and picking bamboo shoots. Some places still had flames licking up.

When we arrived we stopped and had a little rest. Then I filled some water in my bamboo bottle from the stream. We started to explore and a short while later Noy pulled out a huge bird burnt in the fire. Then a big rat. I kept on searching and finally found a small deer laying there, all the fur scorched off. I picked it up and kept on searching while dragging the deer behind me.

I heard my sister scream and ran to her. There I saw a big porcupine, still moving. It must have come in from the forest nearby. This type had sharp quills and he could shoot us with them. I shouted at Noy to keep away and tried to hit it with a stick but he shot his quills. One hit my left leg. Luckily, it wasn't too deep. The porcupine tried to escape but I was quick enough to chase it. I hit it hard with my stick and finally killed it.

We dragged the dead animals we had found down to the stream and cleaned them. I cut some jungle vine and tied the deer and the porcupine together and carried them on my back while Noy carried the smaller animals, heading for home quietly behind me. It was all very heavy but we were happy. When we got home Mom and my brothers were happy too. Mom ran down and helped me carry the animals up to the house. Noy and I were were covered in dark charcoal, head to toe, our faces black with soot.

We had a rest and bathed in the cool river and when we came home we had a big meal together. Mom had cooked the venison and it was delicious.

Our haul of food lasted us for nearly two weeks.

Harvesting Meng Ee

Meng Ee is a Khmu word for an insect similar to a cicada. Around the beginning of April, a few days after the field burning, villagers flock to the forest to cut dry bamboo in order to make a fire lamp for harvesting the Meng Ee. The harvesting season only comes every five years. Because of its rarity and the delicious taste it is a good cash crop so villagers try to make a lot of money out of it. Not every field has such bugs coming out after the burning — only thick bamboo forest and hilly farmland.

One morning we all left for the farm to clear up the leftover stalks and bush from burning so we could plant rice and other crops. The walk took us about an hour.

This time of the year is very hot but also beautiful, the mountain tops stretching in a heat haze, one to another. Much of the farmland smells fresh from burning and being left a few days for the smoke to clear. New shoots break through.

On our way we came across some other families working hard in their fields. We could hear the children cry in the huts high on the mountain, their parents yelling at them. Other kids were busy fetching water from the stream to bring up to their huts in bamboo bottles. We too stopped at a small pool in a dip in the land to fill up with some water and clean ourselves, sipping from the cool running stream.

We were renting our bit of hilly farmland from a family in the village because our own land was not yet good enough for crops. Any farmland has to be left fallow for at least three years before it can be farmed again. The soil needs time to restore itself and also holds more moisture after being overgrown with grass for several years. As compensation we paid this family in rice after the harvest. No rice and we would have had to pay in cash, which we didn't have.

Ten minutes later and we reached the hilltop where we had decided we would erect our bamboo hut for that year. Mom, Sone and Nid marched off to the edge of the field where all the big bamboo trees were, each with a big machete.

Noy and I set a fire and prepared breakfast. We had brought some leftover food cooked the night before and also picked wild vegetables along the way. It was enough.

While we were cooking we could hear the sound of trees being cut far away, along with the birdsong. The atmosphere was beautiful and fresh.

Soon the three others brought back big piles of bamboo and wood and we were able to enjoy our breakfast. Then they started to build our hut, hammering down the stilts first. Mom asked me and Noy to go pick some more wild vegetables and young bamboo shoots for lunch.

We brought our little bag and a knife down the hill to the stream where we had sipped fresh water but then continued on, gathering vegetables as we went. We entered others' farmland and poked about nosily. Soon we had enough and decided to return to our farm. On the way Noy caught a young Meng Ee. The bug's wings were emerging prior to flying away. Then she caught another, and another. By the time we got back to the family our hands were full of Meng Ee. We fried them and they tasted so good!

Mom reminded us that this was one of those infrequent seasons when these special creatures emerged and that if we were not too tired we should stay up late so we could collect a full harvest of succulent bugs.

The day passed quickly and evening fell. Sone was most enthusiastic about finding the Meng Ee. He and Nid fetched dry bamboo to set a fire for later in the night, then, around midnight, we lit it, made torches and each of us armed ourselves with a big bamboo 'bottle' for holding any catch we could make.

Mom and Noy went one way and us three boys another. The moment we directed the flame downwards startled bugs rose, swarming up from the ground. Enticed by the light they clambered their way up the stalks to release their wings.

We grabbed as many as we could. And pretty soon all of our bottles were full. And now, well past midnight, all the hills around us glowed white as the young bugs' wings, still too immature to fly off, fluttered like stars mirroring the starscape above.

We decided to walk all the way home with our belongings. Sone led the way and Mom took up the rear. The dry bamboo lamps were bright enough to lead us home safely. It was a bit scary as we passed little caves and streams along the way, but we got back in one piece. In the gloom of the night forest, it took us much longer than an hour.

Next morning we cleaned the bugs and steamed them in a bamboo basket. We ate some and dried the rest for later. They were tender and crispy after frying.

When evening came me, Nid, me and three other boys from the village headed off to collect more bugs. This time it was a bit messy because none of us wanted to lead the way or be at the back because we were all too scared without an adult in charge. Khmu believe that the ones at the front and the back are more likely to see a ghost and lose their souls. Such profound sickness could follow that it might soon lead to death.

So we made a deal. Whoever was at the back or leading the way would get an extra portion of our bug harvest. We hesitated with our plan until the two oldest boys volunteered to take on the responsibility, so they got extra helpings at the end. We arrived home really late that night but we had lots of juicy Meng Ee. The crop fed us for several days.

Learning to fish

Our lives improved as farming season gathered pace. Sone made more friends who liked to go out hunting with him. He was able to replace Dad at least for that. Mom, Nid, me and Noy took care of the farm and the chores.

I first went fishing when the rainy season started that year. Mayflies emerge after the downpours, and kids and adults know it's time to head for the river to go fishing. Noy and I were eager to join in so we bought a fishing hook and ran around gathering up mayflies. They come up out of little holes in the ground once they feel the dampness.

When we had enough we went off to the river in our little bamboo hats, to protect ourselves from the rain. We threw our hooks in the water on their string and began to fish. It was a lot of fun. The fish were plenty, although very small.

After about an hour we had more than 20. My sister had to run back home to get a bigger basket so we could catch some more. By evening time we had enough for a big meal. I steamed the fish in banana leaves with herbs. When my Mom and brothers arrived home from the farm they were surprised and happy. After working through the heat of the day, coming home to a hot meal meant they didn't have to worry about what to eat.

After that Noy and I went fishing almost every time it rained. Sometimes we walked along the riverbank up as far as we could go, so that nobody was around. We enjoyed the quietness and the sound of the rain as we pulled in our catch.

Sometimes we spent the whole day fishing and only came home late in the evening. For those days we had to bring rice and chili paste along with us and a match to light a fire. Then we cooked some of the fish we had caught for a healthy fresh lunch along the river bank, me nearly nine and Noy just five, fending for ourselves, the forest stretching for miles around us. We learned so much.

One evening after the rain, me and my brothers decided to borrow our neighbour's boat. They were a nice family. They allowed us to sail off, but if we caught some frogs we had to share them as compensation. It seemed fair enough to us. We prepared a lot of dried bamboo to make a torch.

Leaving home in the early evening we rowed the boat upstream as far as we could go. Around midnight the frogs began to emerge for their food. I was in the back of the boat, rowing gently to keep our balance. Nid was near the front holding the craft close to the bank. Sone in the middle held the lit bamboo lamp in one hand as he used his other to grab the frogs. At night they barely move, squatting there, so it's easy to catch them. In a few hours we had filled our big bamboo baskets so we returned home well satisfied.

Mom hadn't slept, waiting for us to return. She was happy with our catch. She placed a heavy wooden tray on top of the bamboo basket so the frogs couldn't escape and we went to bed.

The next morning Mom woke up early and washed and cleaned the frogs, with Noy helping her out. We handed over a lot to our neighbour who had allowed us to borrow the boat.

Japanese gift

The district around Nong Keo has relied on the Nam Nga as a water source for everyday life and irrigation for generations. Our village also has a few little streams running down from the steep hills nearby. In dry season the big river is convenient for villagers to bathe and dip in after coming back hot and sweating from the farm. Every evening the women and children carry big baskets full of clothes down to the water for washing, then fill buckets of it for cooking, drinking and feeding the animals. During flood season though, the big river becomes very dangerous because of its strong current. It becomes putrid and filthy, so most people switch to the little streams instead.

The small streams are convenient for those coming back from the farms. They walk past on their way home and stop to bathe and clean their dishes. They are cooler and cleaner so most people use them for drinking water even though they are a little way from the settlement.

One day a girl was raped on her way back to the village from getting water at one of the streams. The man was caught and fined as well as shamed for what he did. Since that incident people became very afraid of allowing their children, especially the girls, to go fetch water.

Also a rumour was passed on from the village near the main road saying that a gang of Chinese men had come to the countryside bringing candies that they used to lure the kids. Then they kidnapped them and killed them for their organs. Everyone was afraid of this. Nothing happened, despite the rumour, but it took quite a while before life returned to normal and people were comfortable going out without worrying.

In June a Japanese couple arrived unannounced at my village with a tour guide. They walked around and tried to interact with local people. Many kids came around to gawp at them, including myself. The pair talked in Japanese and the guide translated and then they asked if they could talk to the village chief. Someone went to fetch him and they talked together about possibly helping the village out.

Then they left for the city.

About two weeks later they came back as they had decided they'd build us a water pump to make life easier. Soon two boats arrived crammed with construction workers as well as managers to run the project.

One evening after dinner someone rang a bell

and everyone gathered. We began a long, outdoor conference with a big fire in the middle. The village chief read instructions and informed people what we had to do to help with the project. Everyone was happy, cheering and clapping.

Every family had to carry three bags of cement from the pier up to the construction site as well as ten bags of sand and another ten bags of stone.

Next morning the boats came and people flocked to the pier to load the cement. It was heavy so youngsters like myself couldn't carry the bags. My Mom brought her own big bag and loaded one bag of cement into it each time.

Then my brothers and other families took the boat and paddled downstream to load the sand and stones. I helped them carry some of the sand from the pier up to the village using a little bag Mom had sewn for me to carry vegetables and bamboo shoots.

From a stream higher up, we dug a long channel for a pipe all the way down to the village and fed it into a main tank. From there smaller pipes were added to set up outflows. Three weeks later and everything was done. Now we have 11 water pumps in the village. The managers told us we needed to keep them clean and take good care of them, and from then on water supply was no longer a chore.

We killed a water buffalo to celebrate our gift and invited our sponsors, the Japanese couple. We organised a Baci ceremony for them and wished them luck and thanked them for helping us out. They were happy, smiled with satisfaction and took lots of pictures.

Severe illness

Two months later, just after planting season had finished, I fell very ill. No one knew why. My Mom thought that Dad's spirit was trying to take me away with him. For more than a month I could barely walk. All I could do was lie in bed. My family became very worried.

I got skinnier and skinnier. My Mom tried her best with traditional medicine. Sometimes she asked the shaman to come and perform a ritual ceremony. It didn't help.

Two months passed. My health got no better. Mom had to stay at home most of the time to take care of me. The farm became overgrown with incessant rain. My two brothers' hard work was not enough to clear it out. Soon, more than half of the vegetables and rice had been destroyed. We could see that we would be facing starvation over the coming year.

As my sickness failed to improve my Mom became tired of taking care of me. Many times I heard her complain. One time she wished I were dead. It made me very sad and hurt me to hear my Mom wishing me dead. It was her pain and frustration.

My head became swollen after the wound from the machete attack became infected again. Everyone in the family thought I'd die. I thought I would too. One evening Mom knelt down and prayed to Dad, asking him to take good care of me when I'd gone.

Next day she fed me rice soup, spicy chicken and green mango. Usually people don't feed the sick with this kind of food because they believe they will die from the oil in the chicken and the sourness of the mangos. These ingredients often make people more sick. But in my case, since my Mom thought I wasn't going to survive, she had decided to feed me whatever I wanted. She thought that it might be my last time I would have to enjoy what I liked.

That evening we received a surprise visit from Meuan and her husband. It had taken them nine hours to walk from my grandfather's village. It was even more of a surprise though that they came with all their belongings. We soon found out that they were coming to live with us because life with my grandfather had become too hard. He had used them to do all the hard work but he never gave them anything in return. Not a penny, even when they were leaving.

They brought us cucumbers and corn. Meuan came to me in the bedroom and left me with a smooth little cucumber. I was able to eat it later.

Next morning I found I had some energy. I was able to crawl from my bed and out of the house. My Mom was overjoyed to see me crawling. She took me out and cleaned my face by the balcony and fed me some food.

Several weeks later I started to get better but my head was still a bit swollen. I'd lost my hair where the swollen spot was. Kids laughed at me every time I came out, sniggering at how skinny I was. My flat butt was a joke too.

It took me a long time to recover and get back to normal. It felt a like a miracle that I had survived at all. It had been a nightmare but we pulled through. "If I survive this pain," I thought to myself, "I will live for eternity." Having my sister and her husband with us made our lives a little easier. They helped a lot with the hard work. So once again our lives improved.

An old love returns

Around mid-August merchants often come to my village to sell clothing and other goods. They come during the holidays, before school starts, because the villagers, including the children, are all at home.

My village still had no school but some parents sent their children to classes in a Lao town about two hours walk away. The young ones stayed in a dormitory during the week and came back home on the weekends to help their parents with work about the house and farm.

One late August morning a young woman arrived in my village with her husband to set up a temporary stall, a sort of pop-up store. The villagers flocked to them to check what they were selling. Some bought school uniforms for their kids, others casual clothing for themselves.

Noy, Mom and I were among those in the store. We came back home without buying anything, but in the late afternoon, as people began to leave, Mom went back because she wanted a skirt for herself.

She had had a chance to talk to the seller, asking her where she came from and what she did for a living apart from selling clothes. The young woman replied that she lived in the south of the district, around three hours away by bus.

She added that her father used to come often to our village when he was young, to sell clothes, along with his parents. It was when he was around 22 or 23 years old. It was then that he had found a woman with whom he had fallen in love. He had nearly married her.

My mother's heart began to pound.

The young woman continued: "At that time, my father and his parents lived nearby, but when my grandfather passed away my grandmother and father decided to move out. They came to their new village. And it was there that he met my mother."

"And what is your father's name?" my mother asked, warily.

"Sinan," she answered.

My mother stood there speechless. But she said nothing. She felt embarrassed. It would have been too awkward. She would have to tell this young woman, here following her father's old trade, that she, my Mom, was her father's former girlfriend.

"I could have invited her for a meal, but I felt too embarrassed," she told us later. The chance encounter had brought her back to the time when she had been young and single. It was a time when she had been enjoying her life, attractive and beautiful. "My life could have been different if I had listened to your grandparents and married this man instead of your father," she told us.

We could sense that, in some ways, she regretted her decision to choose Dad instead of Sinan. I was left hoping she realised nobody can predict their future. And that she realised she wouldn't have been able to have us if she had chosen Sinan. It was the same thought in all our heads: if she had chosen Sinan we wouldn't have been her children. We didn't dare mention it to her.

Mom's accident

One evening a few months after Meuan and her husband Thongsavath had returned to live with us we had a big party at our house. It was rare to have a party inside, but we were celebrating the successful start of the farming season. We invited many neighbours to come join us. They enjoyed lots of Khmu whiskey from big jars, and a lot of food. A few older women sang Khmu songs, while men played the Khaen, a traditional Khmu instrument made from bamboo, a bit like a flute. It was a fun night with many laughs and smiling, people clapping, drinking and eating until midnight. Finally, the neighbours started to leave and we went off to bed.

Next morning everyone left for the farm except myself. I was taking care of the house and the chickens.

This time of year being the opening of the farming season, every family is busy. It's bush-clearing season. Lots of people head out, the men with their axes and machetes for cutting the taller trees. Unusually, that morning everyone in my family was happy and enthusiastic to start their day.

My brother-in-law and my sister led the way, followed by Mom, Sone, Nid and Noy, and a few other families who would be helping us hack through the forest. They reached the farm in an hour. There my sister and her husband had already prepared breakfast for everyone with food they had brought from home. They had their meal and a rest while my brother-in-law sharpened machetes with a piece of sandstone.

Soon they all left to clear the forest. The land was steep and dense with tall trees and banana plants. My brother-in-law led the group, and they started to clear upwards from low down. Just as Mom was cutting her last tree before heading upwards to where everyone else was standing, Meuan slashed into a big banana tree above her. The heavy trunk collapsed directly onto Mom. It pushed her downhill for many meters, the machete, sharpened for the day's work, still in her grasp. It sliced across three of her fingers, deepest on her ring finger and nearly cutting it off. Blood spurted as she lay on the ground.

Everyone was in shock.

Gathering themselves, the family lifted her up and hurried as quickly as they could down the hill and back to camp. One of the women found some Jidkeo leaves to help stanch the bleeding. Mom rested until the bleeding stopped. Then the unhappy group walked her slowly home.

I was skipping with three other kids near my house. Suddenly I heard a boy call out: "Nat! Your

Mom is back. It looks like she's had an accident!"

I rushed back in and saw her leaning against the wall, pale and exhausted. She had a rope looped round her neck to hold up her right hand. Blood was dripping to the floor. I shivered and felt the pain she was feeling. I rushed into the kitchen, lit the fire, boiled some water and added traditional medicine. I cleaned her wound with warm water. I noticed that her ring finger had nearly come away. She asked to lie down, complaining that she had a pain in her back.

The back pain has lived with her ever since.

She is convinced it comes from a spirit or someone who has cast black magic on her. She offers sacrifices and invites numerous shamans to do their rituals. She never improves. She believes the accident happened because the party the night before caused the spirit in the house to become angry. The spirit was punishing her for making so much noise.

Starting school

A few months later Lae came back to visit us from Vientiane Capital. She suggested to me that I start school, saying that kids in the city all went there. I'd never been interested in it and had never heard much about it so I told her that I wouldn't because I preferred working on the farm. I reckoned I would grow up and be a good farmer and hunter, just like my Dad.

She kept insisting, telling me that if I jojned

school she would buy me some nice clothes and gifts every time she came to visit. I told her I'd have a think about it and maybe it would be better if Nid also joined me. My Mom talked to us one night after dinner saying it was a good idea if we started as it meant we could then be different from anyone in her bloodline. Up to her generation nobody had ever been to school.

The environment and the circumstances we were in wasn't a healthy place for us to grow up and to remain for the rest of our lives. My Mom explained: "The hatred, the bullying and not having the same respect as any other people in the village means it is definitely not a place for us. I want you to be different, go out there, get away from here, get an education and don't end up like me." What she worried about most was that, when she passed away, we would have difficulty making much of our lives in such a place.

I felt sad. Sometimes I felt that she didn't want us to be with her. Now, when I look back, I realise how lucky I was to end up here, sitting in my little apartment room writing this story in English. Most of the kids in the village were told by their parents not to go anywhere; they would have then remained close to home, built their own families and taken care of their parents when they became old and grey. This was the mindset, the acceptable pattern of country people.

I surely would have been a different person if my Mom hadn't let me leave in the first place. I now feel blessed and grateful for my sister who convinced me to go to school. I could have been a farmer, a hunter, a father, or maybe dead from an unknown illness. Who knows? Looking at those kids who still live in the village and the lives they lead makes me sad. Their parents did not educate them the way Mom did us.

Before Lae returned to Vientiane she gave us some money. Two days later Thongsavath, and Nid and I walked all the way down to Nam Nga secondary school in the next big village. It took us four hours there and back. Neither I nor my brother spoke Lao. We were brought into the office and my brother-in-law talked to one of the teachers. At first they rejected us because we were too late. It had been more than three months already since the school year had started. Luckily, the director came and they talked for a bit. Then he said yes.

We registered and over the following days, Meuan and Thongsavath, Sone, Nid and I built a little hut near the school for us to stay in during the week. We moved in, started school and came home each weekend. And that's when I started my journey to become a different person, to leave the village, as my Mom had wanted.

3: Buddhism

Chapter 9

The monastery

The school was very tough for both me and Nid. Rules were intense and strictly enforced. Every Friday we had a test and if anyone failed they were punished. That could involve running around the school yard three times or standing in front of the blackboard and singing to the rest of the class. And with my voice that was embarrassing.

In serious cases when rules were broken, the boy or girl was made to skip a class, or they might be caned, in front of everyone.

It was tough but it helped us to concentrate and try our best. For me it worked well — I learned quickly and did well in a few subjects, except maths. I hated maths.

Within a few months I had slowly learned to speak and understand Lao to an acceptable level and could communicate with my classmates pretty well. The school used Lao in class. That's when I started to make friends. Nid and I came home every weekend. On one of these I took the chance to work with a new friend in the garden near the river in my village. We planted onions, lettuce and coriander. We did this all through the first semester and into the second.

At school one day, another of the friends I'd made in class, who had left to become a novice, returned for a visit. I was fascinated by this boy who'd shaved his head and eyebrows and was covered with an orange robe. He was intriguing and holy!

I didn't know the proper words to use each time we had a conversation. Talking to monks demands a different vocabulary to talking to laypeople. But he was nice and he shared so many things with me about life as a young novice in the temple: the strict rules, the discipline, meditation, eating habits and daily routines.

The most interesting part for me was how many young boys from different backgrounds lived together like brothers, a sort of family, always supporting one another. And I loved that they also studied the Buddha's ancient language of Pali.

We became close friends and after the school break he suggested that maybe I should try to become a monk for a short time.

"In Buddhism, people believe that, by becoming a monk and practising meditation, you can send your late beloved ones to rest in peace," he said. "And so it would be good for you to do it too since your father has died," he added.

I kept this in mind and one night soon afterwards talked to my Mom about becoming a novice.

She didn't know much about it but she said it could be possible because it would only occupy me for three months, during the school holiday.

When we met again I told my novice friend I'd like to try and see how I would like the life. In order to become a novice you have to find a sponsor to support your ordination. It costs quite a bit as the sponsor has to pay for the people who come help to set up and prepare for the ceremony. They also have to buy gifts for the monks whom they've invited for the occasion.

My friend talked to the abbot of Paxieng temple where he lived. Satu Buntan [or Sadhu, a Buddhist priest] asked my friend to bring me along first to see him. This is important because the abbot has to judge whether the boy is mature enough to cope with the hardship and the strict rules set by the temple. Anyone who wants to be a monk has to be at least 10 years old. At the time I was not yet 10. Satu Buntan said I was too young and that I had to wait another year to be ready. I was sad.

Luckily for me, in some exceptional cases they count an extra nine months for when the applicant is in his mother's belly. So, by that reckoning, I was almost 10! Plus, I was mature for my age and I didn't really behave like a child. The abbot relented and accepted me. I came home and talked to my Mom, happy but nervous. That night I didn't sleep.

I would first have to stay in the temple for seven days before I officially became a novice. This was to learn basic rules and simple Pali to pray during ceremonies. So next morning I packed my belongings into a little backpack that Lae had given me as a gift.

Two other boys from my village had also decided to join the monastery at the same time in the same temple. I felt a bit happier because I would have some people to talk to in Khmu at a time when my Lao wasn't that strong.

Trial period

The three of us left early. Down by the river we caught a small public boat. It headed downstream to the main road where it pulled in to the jetty. Then we waited for about an hour before a truck pulled up. We hopped on and headed off.

I felt a bit strange, being away from my family again. And this time I wouldn't even be able to visit my parents, siblings or anyone I knew, a life for myself in a temple, a novel environment for a boy from an animist background. I didn't really know if I'd survive for the three months of the holidays — I'd been missing my Mom from the moment I'd left her. I cried during the two-hour journey on the truck.

When we arrived at the temple my friend brought us up to the hall to meet with Satu Buntan and introduce ourselves once again. We also had to show him the permit from the chief of the village from where we'd come.

It was noon, right after lunch time, but although they had left some food I didn't eat because I was so homesick. The other two boys felt the same.

That night I didn't sleep. Around 4am I heard the sound of the bell being hit by one of the monks or novices. This was a signal to let people know that the new day had started and for the monks and novices to wake up for chanting.

We woke, cleaned our faces and went to the chanting hall. In total we were six novices and two monks. We three new boys sat there listening as they chanted. At first we were very sleepy but that faded away. Maybe the rhythmical, slightly piercing voices kept my eyes open, or maybe the elaborately decorated hall impressed me, but I could feel myself becoming more aware.

After the chanting the abbot turned his face to all of us and told us to learn the basic Pali words for the ceremony. He asked my friend to write it down for all of us.

Around 6 o'clock one of the monks hit the big drum and soon afterwards two of them began to prepare trays. We came to help them out and sat down silently. Soon many elderly women dressed in traditional Lao costumes with sashes draped from their shoulders and carrying boxes of sticky rice and bowls of food walked up the hall and started to offer alms. It was new to me and very beautiful. I liked the serenity and modesty of these ladies offering their rice to the monks. After the offering they asked the other monk at Paxieng, Satu Bun Chan, who we were and where we had come from.

Satu Bun Chan, whom I came to know as Chan, would be my sponsor. He told them about us, mentioning that he would back me while another two families would sponsor the two other boys for the ordination ceremony in the coming days. Those ladies advised us to behave well and study hard and not to be lazy or we would be beaten up by our master.

They laughed. We knew it was a joke.

We sat there watching the monks quietly having their breakfast. My novice friend asked me to go and fetch a bowl of water for the abbot to wash his hands after the meal. Once the two monks had finished it was our turn to eat.

After breakfast we cleaned the dishes, mopped the floor and swept the yard, and then went to study Pali. We all still missed our families and homes a lot. One of the boys complained that it was too hard and too many chores had to be done. I didn't say anything. For me these were the lightest of jobs compared to what I had become used to back in the village. Working on the farm and going out hunting was a lot harder. I had to agree though that in the temple the work was more about mental effort than physical.

Our trial week quickly passed and the day of ordination arrived. My monk friend shaved our heads and eyebrows. The chanting hall was full of flowers along with the beautiful smell of incense and candles. Many people joined us and dressed elegantly in traditional costume.

Satu Buntan and the monks arrived and began to pray. The three of us were behind them, dressed all in white, carrying a plate in our hands with five flowers on each plate.

After the chanting was done, the time for the

ceremony had arrived. I was in the middle and the abbot asked us to come closer. The two families sponsoring the two boys handed robes to the boys. My master, Chan, had mine and he handed it to me. The monks blessed us and performed a ceremony, then asked us to don our orange robes. My monk friend and two others helped us out.

Then we were brought into the hall again and this time we had to say the Pali words that we'd learned earlier. Some parts we had to repeat after the abbot. Soon the ceremony was done and we had officially become monks. Clad in orange and now bald, with no eyebrows, felt weird but that's how it is meant to be. We turned our faces to the people who'd come to join in the ceremony and saw their beautiful smiles. They were happy to see us in our robes.

Then the abbot presented his sermon, telling us about the traditions behind being a monk, what it meant for us and explaining why anyone could become one.

I was sitting there paying attention to him while at the same time being amazed at how I'd transformed from the lay world, and an animist one, to becoming a Buddhist monk in such a short period. As the preaching went on I felt quite unreal.

Novice

Living my new life as a novice came as a big shock and change for me. I had to learn so many things and adapt to so much. For the three of us, starting to learn Pali, waking up at 4am and having only two meals a day were the hardest.

First, we had to learn, and strictly follow, the ten precepts:

1. **To abstain from killing**

2. **To abstain from taking what is not given**

3. **To abstain from sexual misconduct**

4. **To abstain from false speech**

5. **To abstain from intoxicants that cause carelessness**

6. **To refrain from eating at a forbidden time (Noon—1am)**

7. **To refrain from dancing, singing and seeing any form of entertainment**

8. **To refrain from luxurious garments, perfumes and beautifying the body with cosmetics**

9. **To refrain from lying on high or luxurious sleeping places**

10. **To refrain from accepting gold and other high-value objects**

These rules were set out by the Buddha during his time so that his disciples could live humble and simple lives. Apart from the 10 precepts, we also took an oral test every 15 days. The senior monk gave us scripts to learn and recite and, within 15 days, we had to be able to pray without looking at the book. If we failed we were punished with something like having to wash the dishes and clean up the yard for three days. If we failed the same test three times we would be banished.

We also took turns to wake up before everyone else to ring the bell, open the main hall, prepare the chairs and light the candles for morning chanting. We also took turns to clean the dining room and wash the dishes. I liked it this way because we all worked fairly and equally. We lived like a big family. I no longer missed my Mom and my own family.

Soon though came the sad news that my good friend was moving to Vientiane permanently for study. In order to resettle in a new temple he first had to be accepted by them, then he had to receive a moving permit from his current temple. But it all came through for him and it was sad after evening chanting when the abbot declared that he was leaving tomorrow, for good. But it was his choice.

We woke up early and did our jobs like we always did but that morning was different. My friend was packing while I and two others were preparing the trays for breakfast. Soon the ladies came with food and rice to the dining hall. They asked which one was moving to Vientiane Capital. They wished him luck and all the best for his journey. Around 4:30pm I accompanied my friend with his bags to the main road. We waited until the bus arrived from the north, picked him up and drove away. I felt like I had been punched in the stomach. We never got to see each other again after that.

My master's surprise

When the school year was about to start I thought it was a good chance for me to continue my study, but unfortunately Satu Bun Chan decided to move back to his home town where he still had family. In order to resettle in his village and a new temple he had to bring me along.

It was a tough situation because I really wanted to stay in the temple where my two friends were. It was livelier too, near the main road whereas the new place was deep in the countryside and far from anywhere else. I'd miss school too.

It didn't matter what I thought though, because the master needed a novice, so when the time came to move I couldn't do anything except pack my belongings. It was sad for me but at the same time I felt excited when I thought of this remote place. It would be like my home town.

On that morning I woke up earlier than usual. We normally wake at 4am but this time I was up at 3am, if I slept at all. I tossed and turned all night wondering if I would survive in the new place or would I disrobe and go back to my home town for a reunion with my family?

All I kept in mind was: 'OK, what will be, will be.

Let's just move there first and, if the worst comes to the worst and I don't like it at all, I can just disrobe.'

I disliked the idea of disrobing and going back to my village though. My Mom had sent me away for a good reason — this was the only chance I had to make a difference for my own good. The place where I came from wasn't a place I could call home, even though I had been born and grew up there. To me that village was like a curse. Our life there had been full of trouble, hatred and dark memories. I didn't want to regress to that. I felt I had to leave it behind.

I couldn't go back and change the past but I could at least push myself away from it and change the way I felt about it. That morning, after chanting followed by deep meditation, the resolution to my own hesitation had become clear. I knew that my Mom would be very disappointed if I disrobed and went back to the village. I also felt that I had come in the right direction and I should walk to the edge of it. As the darkness slowly turned to dawn I felt more and more confident about my upcoming life in the new temple.

I went to the dining hall to clean and mop the floor, then I set up the trays and hit the drum and returned to the hall. I put on my large orange robe, ready for my last almsgiving ceremony in the temple. I was quiet but my master had a big smile on his face. I could tell he would be happy to see his family again after such a long time away.

Soon all the monks and novices came to the hall with their bowls, sitting and calmly waiting for the ceremony to begin as more and more people arrived with vegetables and rice in their hands. They were dressed beautifully in traditional outfits. Many showed interest in me and my prospective life. They asked how I was feeling: was I ready to move to a new place, would I miss the temple and all my friends? They offered advice too, warning that "there will be only you and your master, so be patient and diligent".

Soon the ceremony started. The abbot walked to the front row, followed by my master and another monk. Then all the novices filled the hall to the back row. I was seated last. We collected alms from the people then chanted a blessing in Pali and offered our thanks to those who had provided us with vegetables and rice. Then we shared our breakfast together.

Only my last cleaning up was left to do. After that I packed my belongings before helping my master with his. The abbot came to see us and gave us little gifts. He offered his blessing and good wishes for us and our lives in a new home.

Then we carried our belongings to the main road where we hopped on a truck and were driven off towards our new home. My novice friends waved at me for the last time. It was the last time I saw them.

Chapter 10

A new home

The journey took us nearly two hours along a muddy, bumpy road. But as soon as the truck stopped I felt like I had been punched very hard in the stomach. It was then that I knew we'd reached our new home. I felt homesick until the end of the day, missing my friends and missing my mother painfully. It was the same feeling as when I first left my village.

Only months before I'd moved to a new place, soon adapting to the new environment and making friends, but then as soon as I started to feel at home I suddenly had to move on. I had to start the process again from zero. Sometimes I didn't know or feel what exactly I was missing.

The driver helped us to unload our belongings from the truck and offered to carry them to the temple. The truck couldn't squeeze in along the narrow road. By now my whole body was covered in the orange dust that had flown into the open truck along the way.

As soon as I saw the temple and the surrounding yard tiredness swept over me. The area was full of overgrown grass and bush. The dwelling hall was dirty and small, just a little bamboo hut. It reminded me of my hometown, and, in a way, that was a small blessing.

But the place itself was cute, isolated as it was from the village, beside a rice field. It had no electricity, but a stream ran nearby where the villagers came to bathe and draw their water. And the main chanting hall was beautiful. Built with cement blocks it had an elegant roof and well-preserved paintings both inside and out showing episodes from the life of the Buddha. Inside the hall was a big Buddha statue in its shelter, sitting serenely. Around it stood and sat many little Buddha statues, left and right, displaying the seven classic poses. The statues still purposefully inhabited their old home in calm repose despite the temple being deserted for a long time.

It's name was Wat Hadkang.

It was nearly noon and as soon as the villagers knew we'd arrived they rushed to the temple to welcome us. It was mostly the older men and women, all dressed in traditional costumes. They brought us food and rice, with big smiles on their faces. One of the ladies was my master Chan's wife. She was humble and friendly. She kept telling me that she had heard about me before and had been waiting to see me in person. My master introduced me to everyone and they were so happy to have their little novice in the village. "You will have to stay here with us and be our next abbot," some joked. They all laughed happily. I sat in front of them, a broad grin on my face, and quickly felt a lot more relaxed than when I had first arrived.

Every village prefers to have monks and novices in their temple rather than leaving it deserted. Having them is a sign of prosperity in terms of spirituality. Traditional Buddhist practice suggests that having a temple and monks bring a feeling of peace to a village. It also offers a chance for villagers to offer food and rice to feed the monks. We call this *Het Boun* which means making merit. It is like an investment for future lives as well as this life. It generates a culture of giving, because we believe that what goes around comes around.

For their part monks and novices are meant to behave properly, to be good and humble, and study the Buddha's teaching as much as they can. They also should perform spiritual exercises and rituals such as chanting, house blessings, funerals and any other ceremonial used in everyday life. Monks and lay people support one another.

Soon after our lunch people offered to clean the temple for us. I set and lit a fire, boiled the water, brewed coffee and offered it to everyone who had come to the temple. Then I unpacked my belongings, made the bed for my master and unpacked his stuff while he held talks with the village chief on plans for what we needed and what could be replaced. My master would be sleeping in the main hall while I had my own place in a bamboo hut. I liked it very much. It made me feel no different than when I had been living at home.

After the cleaning people started to leave for

home, thanking me for the coffee while I thanked them for helping us.

Only my master's wife remained, deep in conversation with her husband. My master called me in to be with him because it is seen as inappropriate for a monk and a woman to be somewhere on their own with no-one else present.

In Buddhist culture individuals can join a monastery at any time and any age and they can also leave or disrobe at any point. So it is not just young boys who like joining temples but also older men. In my master's case he had married and bore five children who all went on to raise their own families. In his later years, after fulfilling his role as both father and husband he found he needed to find peace for himself and to pursue a more spiritual life. His family was supportive, including his wife. They supported one another and remained friends.

Despite the dusty, weary arrival, I found I loved my new place. People were gentle and humble. I felt at home.

Extra responsibility

With only me and my master Chan my new life was full of responsibility. The daily routine itself was challenging as I had to do everything myself, not like in the previous temple where six of us helped out and took turns to do each of the chores.

It was also difficult to learn Pali, the language used for chanting and ceremonies as well as the

Buddha's teaching, to a standard good enough to be able to perform my role during rituals. The Pali script just for a house blessing ceremony consists of more than 30 chapters and each of these is extensive, some being as long as ten pages. I had to be able to recite all of the scripts by rote without recourse to the book.

As well as that, new year celebrations, funerals, new house blessings, robe offerings and ordination ceremonies, not to mention daily chanting, all had their own scripts. Each of these was long, and with many chapters. I also had to learn how to deliver a sermon. This was the hardest part because the sound and tone are quite specific and the language used for this type of performance is in Sanskrit, written on palm leaves — the very oldest form of sermon. Although it was manageable, I was only a ten-year-old boy and felt a lot of pressure.

Apart from all of this I had to conscientiously carry out my daily routine of cleaning, washing dishes, making coffee and tea for my master, doing laundry, sounding the bell each morning at 4am and the drum every seven days for the holy day, lighting candles, clearing bush, and making the fire twice a day (we had no electricity). I lit the fire in the morning after chanting and meditation and at 5pm before evening chanting.

It wasn't an easy life, coping with such responsibility, while also having to keep myself calm and modest and humble as a monk should be. Most monks and novices are able to deal with such stresses only because they meditate so much.

I heard the story of an old monk who had lived

and died at our temple. Villagers nearby said they had seen his spirit around midnight a few times on holy days. Wat Hadkang was a little way from the village, dark and a bit creepy at night. My own little hut was further away again from the main hall, where my master slept. Sometimes, when I woke up in the gloom of the early morning to ring the bell and make the fire I could sense a presence behind me. Maybe it was nothing, my own thoughts.

Candlelight

Having no electricity we had to rely on candles and lamps to find our way around in the dark. I was used to this though because we didn't have power in my hometown either. And living in such a rural area meant the villagers didn't have the resources to support us so we had to make the lighting ourselves.

My master kept the condensed milk cans each time he got through one for his coffee. When we had collected enough both of us made our own gas lamps using the cans and some galvanised steel (normally for the roof) along with a little pipe connected to the main body of the lamp and into which we inserted the wick and poured the fuel. We donated some to villagers who needed them.

I learned how to make candles too. When villagers went hunting they often came home with raw honeycomb. Wanting only the honey juice they donated the beeswax to us. I needed a pot, as well as some straight, hollow bamboo sticks, and wicks which I could tear from my old orange robe.

One morning after breakfast I decided to search for bamboo for candles in the forest. It was chilly and misty but I had a robe large enough to keep me warm. It took a while to walk from the temple to the bamboo forest, so along the way I took a rest and built a fire by a stream. Around me broad farmland was dotted with bamboo huts telling me the property belonged to many families rather than one. Water buffalo grazed over the pastures as a stream flowed gently from a nearby mountain.

The scene reminded me of my grandfather's village with its little houses spread all around the hills and a stream flowing nearby, in the midst of farmland and young forest, cattle and water buffalo chewing the cud and soaking languorously in a muddy pond, children running among them searching out grasshoppers and crickets for lunch. I sat down next to the fire, keeping myself warm. I missed so many things. It was the first time in a long time that I had experienced that kind of feeling again. I missed my family very much, sitting there wondering what would have become of me and where would I have ended up if I had never joined the temple.

It made me curious to find out how my family was doing. It had been quite some time since I had left the village. I'd had no more contact with them. Suddenly, the idea of leaving the temple came to my mind. I didn't like the thought very much. I decided to focus on making candles.

I walked on to the forest and chose some straight medium bamboo, neither too big, nor too small. The moment I cut into the bamboo I was startled as two birds flew up from nearby. I had scared them away. I went to check on the ground and saw four little eggs laying sweetly in their nest. I didn't touch them.

My hunting instinct was still with me. The eggs reminded me of when my brothers and I hunted and set traps. And this time, were I not a novice, I would also have set a trap and caught the birds. Remembering what my master had told me, however, sparing the life of all living beings was one of the principles a monk or a novice should have.

"The most basic fear that exists in all beings is our fear of death. We all love our lives," my master had told me once. The two birds flying away, to the point of leaving their eggs behind, showed me how much they feared being harmed themselves.

Returning to my task, I cut enough bamboo to make our candles and decided to walk back to the temple to prepare our lunch. When I arrived it was nearly time to hit the wooden bell and let the villagers know that it was time for our lunch. Soon a few elderly ladies dutifully arrived carrying vegetables and rice.

After our meal I made the fire, boiled the beeswax, cut the hollow bamboo tubes neatly, and placed them vertically on the ground. Then I created a wick holder using bamboo skewers that were long enough to span horizontally across the pipe and tied the string in the middle of the skewer. I tied a pebble to the other end of the string to keep it straight. Then I poured the beeswax into the bamboo 'bottles'. A few hours later I had beautiful candles for chanting. I also gave some to those ladies who needed them.

First invitation

As a novice or monk you are expected to be good at what you do and at how you live your life. People forget a monk or a novice is also a human being with characteristics like anyone else. The difference is that being a novice means you also live your life according to a rule, the monastic law: you must live a simple life, study the teaching, and dress in the orange robe.

One morning after breakfast and cleaning I decided to read a book. It was the story of Prince Siddhartha, the Buddha. It described his journey searching for the noble truths and how to be free from suffering.

It was cold and cloudy. While I was reading and falling intensely into the story I heard my master's voice calling from inside the hall. He wanted a cup of coffee. I went to set the fire and boil the water. While I was busy preparing his drink an elderly man approached me. Asking where the master was, I told him he was inside the hall. The man headed towards it holding a plate with five marigold sticks and wearing a white sash off his shoulder. This had all the signs of an invitation, and it made me nervous.

Soon I had made the coffee and brought it to the hall for my master. I entered as the man was addressing him and heard him talking about having a house blessing some time over the next four days. He would invite both of us and another two monks and two novices from a temple nearby.

Soon after he left, my master wrote down the titles of the scripts that would be prayed at the ceremony. He asked me to recite them all. He said I should be able to repeat everything even before the ceremony started. His instructions demanded more than ten scripts. It was not funny. Each of them was at least a page long. I'd learned and been able to recite nearly half of them, but I still felt a lot of pressure to master the rest of them before the deadline.

So as not to embarrass myself in front of everyone at the ceremony I studied hard. Instead of waking up at 4am I made it 3am instead, silently reading the scripts to myself over and over again, then reciting them, section by section. A couple of days later, after chanting, my master tested me by having me recite all the scripts, which he had laid out in front of him, and without me glancing at the book. I did well at first but, being nervous, I skipped some parts and he demanded that I start over again. I forgot again. Started again. And again, until I could finally recall them all without prompting. It was nearly midnight by the time I finished. I returned to my room in tears.

Finally the big day arrived and a truck went to pick up two monks and two novices from the nearby temple. For me it was the first time in a long time to see other monks and novices. It made me feel good to have new friends to talk to. We asked each other about life in each of our temples.

Soon we all headed to the house where the ceremony was to take place. Many people had arrived in traditional costumes with sashes draped from their shoulders, smiling and greeting us as we arrived. Some had prepared food dishes while others had contributed flowers.

The ceremony began and we all chanted as one. I sweated profusely, but the event was going well. Older women smiled and showered me with praise, saying my voice was beautiful and sharp. They would say that though — I was living in their temple. My master told them I was a quick learner. They said, again, that I should be their next abbot. I smiled.

The ceremony soon finished, we had our lunch, villagers offered us gifts and we walked back to the temple. In an hour the truck came and picked up the four other monks and novices and drove away. I felt sad again having to be alone.

Boun Kao Jee

The end of December is a time for villagers to relax at home after harvest. In Buddhist culture the year can't end without celebrating with a rice cake festival. It has a long history going back to the Buddha's time. In Lao we call it *Boun Kao Jee*. It is celebrated at full moon or on the main Buddhist holiday. Monks and novices shave their heads and eyebrows, and spend a long evening chanting and meditating. Novices are reminded of the precepts by the abbot.

Being brought back to the precepts means that, whatever rule a novice breaks, the infringement is forgiven and the novice can start again. But exceptions arise.

If, on the one hand, one is caught for breaching a minor rule — such as eating after noon — the novice is seen as breaking a rule that carries only a mild punishment for infractions. He will be put to cleaning the yard and doing the dishes for three days, but without being banished.

If a novice engages in sexual misconduct: he will be kicked out immediately. This rule is strictly enforced.

My master and I were busy preparing what we needed for the festival. On full moon day he shaved my head and eyebrows. I did the same for him. After evening chanting I sat in front of him to be brought back to the precepts. He followed this with a short sermon. Then he instructed me on loads of chores that I had to do next morning before we would leave for the forest to cut firewood with all the villagers. Shortly afterwards three older men came to talk and make plans for the festival celebrations with my master. I served them coffee.

We woke up as early as usual but this was different from other days. After our breakfast a truck came with two older monks and four novices from the nearby temple. They were here to join us for the festival. I remembered them from the time they had come for the house blessing. It was thrilling for me because at last I had friends with whom I could talk. Around 9 o'clock all of us monks and novices led the way into the forest, the villagers following behind with all the food and cooking equipment for lunch.

When we arrived at the place, I and four other novices prepared seats for the monks. They themselves engaged in conversation with the older villagers about the structure of the festival. Soon young men and women set out into the forest to chop down trees. Older people set the fire and prepared food for everyone. Some made dessert. We five novices prepared trays and bowls.

At 11 o'clock all the young people had returned to the clearing laden with wood. They took their places to listen to my master preaching. He told them all the story behind the festival, what the celebration was about and why we had it at all. Everyone sat quietly and paid attention. Soon our lunch was carried in. We prayed, and gave a blessing over the food. We ate first and were then joined by the villagers. It was so much fun picnicking with everyone, like a big family. There were lots of smiles and laughter. I realised how much I missed that.

The last part of the festival season was to host a big party at the temple 15 days later. It is held to raise funds for the temple. The entire village put money together to buy the food and supplies. No alcohol was allowed.

Loud music was played and all the villagers came and ate and partied. Around 3am everyone built a big fire with the firewood they had gathered and made rice cake with eggs as well as other recipes. They offered some to the monks in an almsgiving ceremony. Three monks and five novices in total were in attendance. The money was handed over to the temple that had sent out the invitation with some also for us. We used it to lay a wall and do some other building works.

Another surprise

It had been a slow seven months living with my master. I'd passed many tests and progressed well to the next level. Many topics were still left to learn but I was no longer at a basic level.

One evening, after chanting, one of my master's sons came to the temple to talk to him. I was in my room reading a book while they talked. About an hour had passed when my master called me in. "Listen," he said to me very seriously, "I'm leaving the temple (disrobing)."

This was shocking news for me. I hadn't expected it at all. But his family needed him.

"Your Mom is ill," he told me. ('Mom' in this case was his wife. I sometimes called him father.)

His children were busy with their farm and she needed someone to be at home supporting her. So my master was leaving the temple for good.

The only problem now was me. He was concerned for me, so he came up with the options that he could either send me back to the previous temple at Paxieng from where we had moved seven months ago, or I could move to the one next to ours since my master and the abbot knew each other well. I spent most of the next few days thinking about my future, pondering what I might do next.

Each day my master would visit his family and check on his wife. In fact his wife didn't want him to leave the temple because she knew he was happy living the life of a monk.

The days slipped by quickly. Finally, I decided to move back to the previous temple two weeks before my master disrobed. We went there together because he was planning his disrobing ceremony there anyway. It would be on a full moon day and he was going to need at least five senior monks to be witnesses and to perform the ceremony.

It was time to pack again. I felt sad because I'd connected with the villagers and the environment there. On the last day in my beloved temple in the morning for the almsgiving ceremony many people came to offer us rice and other food as usual but this day felt different. They had also come to say goodbye.

They all said they wanted me to live there on my own and they would find a monk from somewhere sooner or later. I was too young though to be in charge of everything. I told them I needed to continue school. They understood.

It was emotional as I said goodbye to everyone. They wished me luck and told me to "please do not forget us, and we hope you come visit us some day". I knew I wouldn't come but I didn't tell them as I gave them a smile.

After lunch and cleaning up we carried our bags and all our belongings to the dirt road. Soon the truck came. We hopped on and drove away once again.

Novice

Chapter 11

A monk

We arrived at Paxieng around lunch time. To my surprise, all the novices who had lived there before had already left. Some had gone to Vientiane, while some had gone back to their families. There were new faces, very young. They didn't do the work the way they should. And I soon discovered that two of the young novices were the abbot's grandsons.

I was speechless and felt depressed. I had been very happy to be back, hoping to meet my old friends, but it had not turned out that way at all. I was not enthusiastic about anything for the first week. The only thing in my head was that soon my master would be gone and I would be there with only the new novices. The idea of returning to my family resurfaced.

It had been so long, with no contact, no news from them. All I hoped was that they were doing well even though I knew what life was like for them.

One day an older man came to the temple with

his truck and some flowers in his hands. He asked me where the abbot was. He was there to invite the monks for a ceremony.

Next morning after breakfast and doing some cleaning my master told me to prepare for a house blessing ceremony. "The truck will come pick us up around 9am," he said.

I was excited because at least I had something to do to distract my mind. At 8:30 I put my large orange robe on and sat in my room waiting for a call from my master. Soon the truck came and I fetched my master's bag and we hopped into the truck and drove towards the town. The place was close to Luang Prabang and nine monks and nine novices had been invited to the ceremony. It was my first time at such a big event. Lots of people joined in too. A loudspeaker made for a dramatic start and the chanting started soon after.

An older monk from a nearby temple took particular interest in my voice. He kept staring at me. I felt uncomfortable, as if I'd done something wrong. In fact, he was just entranced with the accuracy of my voice.

After the ceremony he asked me from where I came and for how long I had been a novice. I told him everything. My master joined in, telling him that I was a quick learner and studied hard while also mentioning that he was leaving Paxieng soon and hoped I'd continue with my good work.

The elderly monk realised I was in a state of transition and asked if I would be interested in moving to his temple. He had only two novices and one was about to leave soon so he needed someone to replace him. I didn't say yes immediately but I knew I'd love it.

We returned to Paxieng after the ceremony and I had completely new thoughts. I was happy with the idea of moving closer to the town and also of enrolling at the school.

Three days later, after breakfast, I asked my master if I could visit the elderly monk and see what the temple there was like.

I packed my bag and walked to the main road. Soon I hopped on a truck and it took only 20 minutes to get there. I was surprised at how nice it was. They had a big dog too. The abbot and I had a long conversation. I joined him and the novices for lunch, did my share of the cleaning, and said my goodbyes. But yes, I'd be moving there! That's what I repeated to myself as soon as I left.

I arrived back at my temple and told my master and the abbot there that I would be moving next morning. It was time to say goodbye once again. My master didn't say much apart from wishing me luck. He told me to keep up the good work and to take care of myself.

Next day after breakfast I left with all my belongings and with a big smile on my face.

Don Mai

I moved to Don Mai temple, just a month before Buddhist Lent, in June. Not long afterwards the novice who was leaving disrobed. It was perfect timing for me to learn and adapt to my new home.

And at least there were two of us now. The temple was larger than the previous one too.

What made this place special was the abbot himself, Satu Sumdhi. He was lively, chatty and smiled a lot. He had married and had two kids and decided to join the temple after this wife had died eight years before. Because I and the other novice were good at what we were doing he didn't have to worry much about imposing the rules or how to take care of us. We would wake up and get into our routine of chanting, cleaning and whatever else without our master having to remind us.

We received too many invitations though. Up to three a day, including house blessings, funerals and offerings, all in different places. Sometimes we left in the early morning to have breakfast in a host's house and and only got back to the temple in the late evening. It could be exhausting. Our abbot had to go to every event, while I and the other novice took turns accompanying him. Sometimes we came back to our temple with no energy left and were allowed to skip the evening chanting. Whoever remained at the temple had to do the chanting on his own.

I disliked praying alone. It could be very tiring. Every time when I stopped to take a breath no-one chimed in to continue the line. Sometimes I forgot what I was going to pray or even mistook the scripts. I laughed alone.

And whoever stayed behind in the temple also had to feed and bathe the dog. His name was Bee, the big guy. I hated the bathing part — Bee was bigger than me. Every time I tried to splash water on him he would shake his body vigorously and wet me as well. He didn't appreciate the exercise either.

Buddhist Lent stretches from July to September, a three-month period when monks and novices aren't allow to travel or spend a night away from the temple. If they go anywhere they have to return and sleep in their monastery unless they fall ill and need urgent care and have to stay in hospital.

Lent has a long history going back to the Buddha's time. This three-month period is the rainy season and it is a time when villagers plant their rice and other crops. Before lent was instituted, monks had often been on pilgrimage around this time. Travelling from place to place, they had to search for a spot in which to hide from the rain and meditate. They travelled during the night and they would accidentally tread on or walk over people's fields where the crops were taking root. This caused so much damage and consternation for the farmers that the Buddha established a rule not allowing monks to leave the temple at all at this time of the year.

Other rules are stricter too during Lent. A monk should not be absent from morning or evening chanting or he will face punishment. However, it happened twice when all three of us slept straight through until dawn without anyone ringing the bell. Two of us were supposed to take turns to wake up at 3:30am to ring it, open the hall, light the candle and prepare the seats for chanting. This time though, I forgot to set the alarm and none of us woke up, not even our master. When I finally roused myself it was already 5 o'clock and I saw my master wiping the steps. I rushed to the bathroom, cleaned my face, threw my robe on, went to clean the dining hall and put all the trays out to prepare for breakfast. Then I sat on the step feeling fat and guilty while watching my master cleaning himself and my friend waking up and slowly trundling to the bathroom.

But no punishment came my way. I think my master understood. But I felt so bad. I knew what to do. I punished myself by cleaning the yard and doing the dishes alone for a day. And my master pointedly remembered to tell me, after evening chanting, not to forget to set the alarm.

Come the start of September all the kids from the village walked past my temple in their school uniforms. The school is just behind our wall. I was very excited too because I was going to register. My master asked me after breakfast if I was ready for school or not. "Of course I am," I replied. He gave me some money to pay for the fees and school supplies.

I went to the principal's room and asked to register. But they asked me to show them my previous record, and which grade I was in. "Damn," I muttered to myself.

First of all I hadn't kept my record. Secondly, even if I had I probably wouldn't show it to them because I had only been in first grade but here I was registering for fifth grade. I was supposed to be registering for grade two. But I couldn't do that as I was too old, having started school late.

My heart was pounding when one of them said: "Sorry, we won't allow you to register without your previous record." I was speechless, but then one of them said: "Never mind, we can allow you to register but you have to bring your record before the first semester." I felt relief but worried at the same time.

Still, I was in, and I duly started school. To my surprise I didn't find the classes too difficult despite jumping from grades one to five. Over the past few years I'd learned a lot anyway. I could read pretty well although I was still poor at maths.

Satu Chan

A year passed in my new home. School finished and for the next stage of my life I knew I had to move to the town where I could join the Buddhist High School. This time I would have to make my own journey. Every day after breakfast I had to walk for more than two hours into the town, then wander around from one temple to another to ask if they needed another novice. It was not easy because each of the temples had at least 25 or 30, or even more, novices and monks. None had spare space. But the school year was getting closer which made me nervous. If I missed the start I would have to wait until the following year.

One day I came to one called Wat Phon Sa-at near the Nam Khan river. It was full of scrub and a large area was covered in long grass. It needed to be cleaned up so, yes, they needed more novices. I went in and asked one of them how many lived here. They had only six and two monks. I continued on to the abbot's room. I paid my respects and asked him if he needed another novice. He said yes.

I immediately felt huge relief and was full of joy that I had finally found a place after so long trying. The route to school meant crossing the river by boat but I didn't care as long as I had found a place and was able to continue my schooling. That is all that mattered.

Before I left I asked for his phone number in case I needed additional information before I moved in.

I came back to my temple feeling so happy. I told Satu Sumdhi that I'd found a place and was ready to move on for my next step. He was very quiet when I told him that. It was emotional for all of us after we had lived together for so long. Now I was about to leave.

I told him that I would be moving out within a week. In the meantime I'd try my best to clean up the temple and tidy the fence and surroundings. I explained how I appreciated the place that had given me shelter and food to eat and especially the master who loved me like his own child.

Three days before I moved out we were invited to a house blessing ceremony 40 minutes drive away. There I met my first master, Satu Bun Chan. I was shocked as I thought he had disrobed already. Seeing him I was speechless. But when I was just about ready to speak up the praying started so I had to wait until the ceremony had ended.

"You have grown up a lot," he said then.

I smiled.

"I thought you had left the temple," I replied.

Our conversation was emotional, and became sad when I learned that his wife had passed away just two days before he was about to disrobe. Because of that he had decided to remain as a monk and dedicate himself to his late wife instead. The children were old enough to take care of themselves. His youngest daughter had just married so there was nothing more he had to worry about. He had also decided not to move back to his hometown.

He asked me if I would be interested in moving back with him. I told him I'd love to but I had to continue my studies and was about to move to the town. Before we left for our temple he gave all the gifts he had received from the ceremony's host to me and wished me luck in my future and in whatever I did. I promised I would come visit him when I had time. I didn't manage this until 2013 after I had left the monastery. I returned only to find that he had passed away in 2009.

The teachings and all that he had given me still remain at the bottom of my heart. He had been like a second father who gave me the affection and warmth my father never could.

Wat Phon Sa-at

Wat Phon Sa-at started well but it was exhausting because I had to study and come back to the temple to clean away all the bush as well as doing the regular daily routine. What made it fun though was living with six other novices and making friends with them. Soon we all became like one big family, eating, praying and working together.

In this temple the abbot, another Satu Buntan, encouraged the novices to plant trees. Because the back of the temple sits on the edge of a cliff overhanging the Nam Khan, when heavy rain falls the ground crumbles slowly into the surging current below. To prevent that we had to plant as many trees as we could because we didn't have the funds to build a concrete wall for protection.

I chose to plant a Bodhi tree because my old master had told me that this species of fig is a spiritual plant. The Buddha is said to have been sitting under such a spreading Bodhi on the night he attained enlightenment. Reposing in its shade in deep meditation he appreciated the circle of life and the suffering that all of us face, including himself. Whoever plants a tree such as this might have a chance to reach enlightenment or even attain nirvana. Or so my master told me.

I planted three of them. One survived. The species is picky and needs good soil to grow well on the bank of the Nam Khan.

Wat Xieng Muan

My life at Wat Phon sa-at didn't last. I had to move again, this time because of its location on the east bank of the Nam Khan. To get to school we had to take a boat across the river but several times the boat sank. It was dangerous when the water level was high and the current strong. We survived each time but it wasn't very convenient, or safe.

I transferred after a year, in May 2010, to another monastery called Wat Xieng Muan in the centre of Luang Prabang. This made going to school a lot easier, as well as most everything else. I was 16 at the time.

This temple was run by Satu Kamla, had 23 novices, four monks, six cats and four dogs. It was quite a big family, which made it lively. I loved every minute of my time there.

After four years there, I was ordained a monk.

Temple

Ordination at Wat Xieng Muan

Monk

Sone

Back in my old family, Nid had left for Vientiane Capital in 2008 to live with Lae and continue his studies. He did construction work during the school break to earn extra money. And later on he too joined a temple to become a novice.

Sone and Noy were still with Mom. But after the harvest season in 2010 Sone and two of his friends from the same village came to Luang Prabang to find construction work. It was his first time in the town. Sone could barely speak or read Lao because he hadn't had a chance to go to school.

The three of them came to town with all their belongings in their big striped ruck sacks, a sign that they were country boys. They wandered around town enquiring until they found work near the old bridge. They were building a new hotel there so they needed more workers.

One morning I got a phone call from Sone saying that he was coming to see me at my temple. It was already a month since he'd been working and so they had decided to go back to the village.

The three of them came to visit me with all their stuff. Poor Sone was so innocent. He was very quiet with a big round head and pale skin. His crossed eyes had become an affectionate joke among his close friends.

That day I decided to skip school and took the three of them to the market instead. I bought a shirt for Sone as a gift which made him happy. He put it on straight away. When I came back to my temple, one of my novice friends said to me: "Look at your brother, how happy he is with his new shirt." I had no idea my brother would appreciate such a little gift so much.

We laughed a little as we watched the three of them walk out of my temple with their big bags. They hopped into a taxi and drove away. I was happy knowing that he was going back to the village so my Mom and Noy wouldn't be lonely. Everything was going well for me, including studying. But soon afterwards, as I was happy in my new place living my life with joy, I received a phone call from Mom. Sone was ill. I told her to get him some medicine. I didn't think he was going to get worse.

Because of her strong belief in Animism, Mom didn't take Sone to the hospital. She could at least have taken him down to the main road to have a check-up because they have a clinic there. But she didn't. Instead she invited the shaman to pray and perform a ritual. This included killing pigs and chickens for a sacrifice.

But Sone still didn't improve. By the beginning of 2011 it was five months since he'd fallen ill. His symptoms kept deteriorating. By now he couldn't move at all. On February 28 Mom called me and asked me to contact Lae in Vientiane to say that she needed K8m (roughly US$900) for a water buffalo to kill for the sacrifice.

The shaman convinced her that if she killed the water buffalo for the spirit then Sone would recover. Mom was blind to her belief. To save Sone she had to get the money as soon as possible. I was angry and tried to convince her to take him to the hospital. She told me it wasn't a disease but something amiss with the spirits. When I called Lae she was angry too. Typical of Lae — she couldn't control her anger and let rip.

But in the end Lae decided to send the K8m to me and asked me to deliver it to my Mom. When I had the money Mom called me to say she had already taken the buffalo and would pay back the owner when I reached home.

On February 30 I left in the early morning for the bus station to go home and deliver the money to Mom. She told me she would walk to the main road and would wait for me to arrive there by bus. Unfortunately, the first bus was full. I had to wait for the second bus, which left at 11am. On the way the bus broke down and it took nearly two hours for another to arrive. I became angry and frustrated.

When I arrived it was already 5pm and Mom had left. I was speechless.

The hunger, the anger and everything else was storming round my head. I had forgotten I was still a novice wearing my orange robe. I decided to run, searching for my Mom. From the main road to my home town normally takes about two hours to walk. I ran and ran and ran, crying at the same time. After about an hour I saw her walking ahead of me, still around 5km from the village. I screamed to her as loud as I could because by then I was spent of any energy. She looked back, turned and walked quickly towards me. She looked skinny and pale. She was sick herself, worn out from taking care of her son.

In her hand she was holding a bamboo bottle filled with snails. She had cooked them for me. When she handed the jar to me I smashed it right in front of her. I couldn't control my anger. But when I looked into her eyes I felt so guilty and emotional while raging with anger at the same time. Instead of going to the village with her I ran back in the direction from where I had come.

I cried all the way until I reached the main road. It was already dark. I cleared my eyes and waited for a bus. An hour passed but still no bus. Two hours. Three. I gave up and walked to a temple nearby, at Ban Nam Nga. The monks and novices had already gone to sleep. I didn't want to bother waking them up. I decided to sleep outside of the chanting hall. It was bitterly cold and I was sad and emotional.

Around midnight I was woken by a soft voice calling Jua, meaning novice. It was one of the novices who had woken up to go to the toilet and found me sleeping there. He brought me inside and offered me a bed. Next morning I left early to return to Luang Prabang.

Three days later my Mom called me saying Sone was deteriorating further. She asked me to come back home and see him. It might be for the last time she said. I told her I wouldn't go because she was having the sacrifice ceremony in the house. They were killing the water buffalo.

But then, after I had thought for a while, I decided to take a taxi to the bus station and hopped on one heading north. When I arrived at the bridge on the main road, it was around 3pm. I was lucky as a boat was about to leave for my village. I embarked and an hour later arrived home.

The moment I jumped off the boat I heard someone crying. The village isn't far from the pier. When I heard the sound of sobbing, my heart began to beat so fast. Approaching, I realised the crying was the sound of my Mom. I was too late. Sone had died a few minutes before I arrived.

The energy drained from me. I was speechless as I walked in and saw his body lying in the middle of our home, all skinny and still in the shirt I had given him. My Mom was just sitting there beside him, sobbing. Noy was with her, in tears.

Beneath the spirit shelter, a shaman sat, still in his costume. I have no words to describe how angry I felt, seeing what was laid out before me. My brother's corpse, my sobbing mother and sister, and a man who had told everyone he could cure my brother sitting there watching the boy's mother grieving for her firstborn son, dead at the age of 23.

If I had a gun I might have shot him in the head there and then. The incident haunted me for a long time afterwards. Like when I was so sick as a child, I told myself that if I could survive this pain I would never die.

I refused to talk to Mom for some time after that. Then I found out from Nid that she too had become very sick. After Lae convinced her she decided that she needed to go to the hospital. I called her to come in to the town and took her to the hospital. They cured her.

I turned completely against Animism. I would never again have any faith in it, or its practices.

Chapter 12

Farewells

Yahern had been a big part of our lives. Growing up in the shadow of domestic violence we found a safe place with her to hide every time we felt threatened, we had food to eat when we were hungry and someone to comfort us when we felt depressed. She offered us not only shelter and food but also mental security. That's something we could never have found back then within our immediate family.

Much later I made regular return visits and she would reminisce about the old days. She recalled especially the day when she led me to Grandpa Ser's village to spread the news about Dad's death and how it took us a day to walk there. It was the day when my family was ruined.

More importantly for her, she recalled the day when Grandpa left us. She was angry with him until the day she died. She complained how he had asked her, Sone, Meuan and Thongsavath to help build the house. It took them nearly a month when they were stuck in his village without seeing their own families. Because no sand was to be had in his village, they had to carry it from far away. And then the cement and concrete had to come from the main road all the way to the village. That took them at least an hour in each direction.

When his house was finally finished he organised a Baci ceremony to bring luck to his home and invited the shaman for the blessing. The following day he gave my brother a bag of rice and some corn, as well as some for my grandaunt. They both then had to walk from morning until early evening to get back to my village. A few days later Sone fell very sick from exhaustion. Mom wasn't happy about it.

Sone complained too until his death about how unfair our grandfather had treated us. Grandpa, on the other hand, took good care of his step-grandson and praised him repeatedly.

Sometimes a good person doesn't get what they deserve. Grandaunt Yahern was one of those. When I was a kid I used to run to her house every time my Dad had got drunk, come home and beat me up, every time when my Mom beat me up, every time when me and my siblings had beaten each other up. Growing up I felt more connection with her than with my own family. It was much safer in her house.

She didn't get what she deserved.

She had her own son and later adopted a baby girl Lid, raising them on her own and giving them their lives in the best way she could. She managed to survive by farming, all the while expecting they would care of her in old age. But neither of them cared enough to take her in when she needed them most. The son married, moved out and set up his own family. Her daughter found a man who at the start seemed good and caring, but then got into drugs and changed completely.

In 2017 Yahern became blind. She was left on her own by her two children. Back when she could see they had used her to take care of their children but abandoned her when she was blind.

One of the villagers came to visit Mom in her new village. She told her the news about Yahern and called me and Nid. As soon as we heard what was happening we came to pick her up from her village and brought her to the hospital in Luang Prabang for treatment.

While she was there neither of her children came to visit her to keep her company. I found their phone numbers and called them, expressing anger for being so irresponsible. Two days later the daughter came to be with her while my brother and I were out working.

Two weeks after surgery Yahern could see again. When the doctor lifted the bandages I was sitting before her. Hesitantly, she asked with surprise: "But what's that on your teeth?" Seeing my new braces was proof enough she could see again.

Before she left hospital I disciplined the daughter a bit, as a monk would a novice. I asked both of them to please take care of their Mom. Nid and I covered the cost of the surgery and gave Yahern some money before she returned to the village.

Two months later we came to visit her and listened to her concern over the work that her daughter had been demanding of her. I felt angry. She had been told to work on the farm and do chores when she was supposed to be recovering.

Before we left the village for the town we asked her if she would be interested in moving to Mom's village. She turned down the offer. So we gave her some money instead. We knew in our hearts it wouldn't go to her but to her son-in-law who was taking drugs.

Seven months later Mom called to tell me that Yahern was very sick. My brother and I rushed back hoping to take her to the hospital. Her children though had already organized a sacrifice ceremony with the shaman. They believed he could heal her sickness. He performed a ritual and later they killed a pig. They offered the blood to the spirit.

The worst moment came when we brought her fruit, vitamins and fresh milk. They told us she couldn't take them because it would make her more sick, or so the shaman had told them. In effect they were starving her. I tried to explain that sick people needed nutrition and proper food to gain strength and energy but still they insisted that she was not supposed to take it. I broke down and cried.

When I held her hand I knew she wouldn't make it. I knew this would be the last time. I could do nothing but cry as I tried to comfort her. She thanked us and heaped praise on us for always taking care of her.

I said: "If this is going to be the last time I get to see you, I wish you all the best for the time that you still have in this world. May you be well and recover soon or, whatever happens to you, I wish that you rest in peace. And may you find a better life to come. At least be in a family where they can take good care of you and not starve you and use you for hard work.

"You're the best, with such a sweet and gentle soul. But you're not lucky enough to have children who would take care of you despite being at this stage of your life. I've tried my best to do whatever I could to save you but, if this is your destiny, then there's nothing I can do about it."

We told her to get better soon so we could come visit again even though we knew she wouldn't get through. We left quickly, as daylight was fading over the village.

My instinct was right. A week later Mom called to say that Yahern had passed away. We consoled ourselves by thinking that, given her great suffering, maybe it was for the best.

Grandpa

In 2009 Grandpa Ser's second wife died and Mom received a surprise visit from him. Tavanh, as we called him by then rather than Ser, walked all the way from his village to ours. But he didn't stay with us. Instead he stayed with his sister Yahern.

In the evening Mom cooked a meal and invited him for dinner with her, Meuan, Thongsavath, Sone, Noy and Yahern. Over dinner he recounted the story of how his wife had died and revealed that his step-son and step-grandson had also left him, taking the fortune that he and his wife had built up from scratch. Only the house, some cattle and farmland had been left for him. He needed people to help him plough the land before the planting season started.

He asked my sister and her husband if they would mind coming to help him out. Thongsavath became angry because he had used them last time to help with hard work and hadn't given them anything when they left. He asked my grandfather: "What about the tractor you bought for your step-grandson? Can't he help you out with that?"

He said he didn't want to talk about it anymore. There was no more connection between them since his wife had passed away. My sister rejected his request. She was angry too.

But after he had returned to his village, my grandaunt and Mom talked to them about it one more time. Finally Yahern, Meuan and her husband decided to go help him out. They stayed there for six days, until they finished the ploughing. After that my grandfather kept coming hack to us, mostly when he needed something. Especially money. He knew that Lae was well off so he he kept calling her and asking. She was generous enough to give him what he wanted until her wealth and relationship started to decline.

When Nid and I had moved out from our monasteries to Luang Prabang he started to contact us knowing we were living there. It was 2013 when I first received a phone call out of the blue from him asking for help. He told me he had gotten my number from Mom. I fondly recalled how he used to take care of me when I was a baby so I decided to give him what he asked for, K600,000 (US$60). I rode from town to his village first along the main, concrete road, then the dirt track. I brought him meat and crackers as well as the money.

Returning to Ban Houy Lae reminded me of my eight-year-old self when I made the barefoot trek from my hometown to the village with Yahern to spread the news about my father's passing.

As I had been a novice not allowed to make visits apart from to home it was my first time seeing him since then. His looks hadn't changed much. When I entered his house he welcomed me with a smile and asked in the traditional Lao way if I'd eaten. I pulled out the meat and crackers and handed him the money, for which he thanked me.

Then he sat down beside the stove, turned his back towards me, and started to talk about how hard his life was. He said he was not feeling well but still had to work hard in the field because no one helped him. And again he brought up the painful past about my parents, what they'd done to him, evicting him and his wife from their own home. I sat there listening to him without saying a word.

I told him I'd go for a walk in the rice field. The place was the same as years before. People still bathed and drank water from the same stream in which I cleaned myself when I arrived there at the age of 8. I walked along, soaked my feet in the stream while refreshing old memories. Then I walked back to the village and wandered around asking people where my friend Vanna was. He was a little boy I met when I came to the village. In the few days I had spent there, we used to walk along the stream, bathing and pretending to catch crabs. I was told he had married a girl from a different village a few years before and had moved closer to her family there.

That evening I rode back to Luang Prabang.

From time to time Tavanh would come in to the town's hospital and give our numbers to the doctors to call us so we would visit him. It was often an unpleasant surprise. He knew that if he had given us advance notice of his stay we wouldn't show up, but if he came to the hospital first and got the doctors to call us then he knew we would. We usually ended up paying his medical bills.

His adopted son had an accident one time and lost one of his fingers. The two of them arrived at Luang Prabang hospital late in the evening and called me in to pay the bill for medical services and the operation. At the time I had only K750,000 (USD75) and I still had to pay my rent and bills while waiting for my monthly paycheck. But because he seemed to need it more I gave him K500,000 and had only the remainder for myself.

He saw us as a money machine even though we were trying to survive ourselves on meagre salaries. Lae and Nid saw what kind of man he had become — they were old enough to know his old self when he was still living with us. It was hard to recall this was the same man who had fought and survived a terrible war, lost his friends and trekked for months through the forest to find his first wife Geud.

Mom reminded me that he used to take care of me when I was a baby. He would take me to his boat when I was crying non-stop in our violent household. That little care he showed me meant I still owed him a lot.

She always asked us to think deeply in regard to Tavanh. Without him there wouldn't be her and without her there wouldn't be us. I found it hard to disagree. As his grandchildren we couldn't let him live in poverty and starve.

He started getting sick more regularly. Sometimes he treated himself at home with traditional medicines and herbs from the forest but he still called us for help with food, meat and whatever else he needed. What could we do? We could do nothing but give him what we had.

On August 7th 2021, well into Covid lockdown, while I was having lunch with Nid, I received a phone call from his wife telling us he was dying and that we needed to come see him as soon as we could. We quickly finished our meal, packed our belongings and went straight to the village on Nid's motorbike. On the one and a half hour journey we stopped to buy food, milk and medicine for him.

When we arrived Tavanh was lying on his bamboo bed without a mattress — it was too humid. He used a Manchester United towel for comfort instead. He was wearing his favorite black shorts and a pink T-shirt Nid had brought him on our last visit. Beside him his third wife was trying to cool him by covering his head with wet cloth. With the effects of illness, age and a lack of good food he has just skin and bone.

We fed him some of the milk, which he sucked through a straw. Then some fruit. An hour later he had regained some energy and began breathlessly talking to us. We could barely hear him with his voice so weak and soft. He insisted on us taking him to the hospital because he didn't want to die.

We had other thoughts. He would surely expire along the way if we did take him as it was such a long distance. There was no car or bus, just our motorbike so that made it even more precarious. The doctors would also refuse to treat him because they would know it was too late. And if he died midway his corpse would not be allowed back into the village because of tradition. Finally, we didn't have the money to pay for it anyway.

In Khmu culture if someone dies away from home their body is not allowed back for burial as it is considered bad luck and a curse. It would put the whole village in danger from evil spirits. If they expired somewhere midway, their body had to be buried near where they died.

We explained this to him as best we could, emphasising what could happen if he insisted on the arduous trip to the hospital. We decided to leave and left him some cash before we headed back for Luang Prabang in the late evening.

Two days later, Mom tearfully called me early to tell me he had died and that we had to return to bury him. Again Nid and I hopped on the bike and headed straight to the village while Meuan and her husband also set off from the north.

Villagers had gathered — but no one was crying. We quickly entered the house and found him laying there, still breathing. He had only passed out but people thought he had died. I had mixed feelings over his resurrection: sadness, anger and hilarity at the same time.

We waited until Meuan and Thongsavath arrived, and explained to Tavanh that he didn't have anything to worry about. If he needed rest and peace he should allow it to himself. I tried to calm him by telling him "this is life and it is how we all end up, when it's time. No one can escape death. When that time arrives, no matter how hard we try to fight against it, no one can defeat our sad and brutal human nature."

I cried a little seeing him fighting so hard to hold on. He was breathing more and more heavily. It was my first time witnessing a death. It reminded me of the Buddha's teaching about the suffering of all beings; that we're in this world only temporarily; there's no such thing as "ageless and forever" for us; we start with nothing and end with nothing, only memories left behind for others to recall.

After a while Tavanh drifted off to sleep. Again Nid and I biked back to Luang Prabang.

Next day I travelled to Vientiane Capital for a UK visa application and to visit Lae. I spent a night with her in her small room and we went out for dinner. It had been a long time. I also took the chance to visit Noy and my niece Onn, both of whom were working in a factory there.

Three days later Lae dropped me to the bus station on her motorbike and I caught the 7:30pm overnight bus. It arrived at 4:45am in Luang Prabang. But just as I was about to fall sleep I received a phone call from my grandmother telling me that Tavanh had died. Definitively this time.

The shaman had arrived to perform a ceremony and was waiting for us to come so they could bury the body. Again on the motorbike Nid and I made our way there.

Tavanh's body was covered in thin old blankets. Next to it was some rice with chicken barbecue and a jar of Khmu whiskey. All for him. We call it 'the meal of the dead'. A bamboo basket beside him was filled with out-of-date banknotes from the Lao Lan Xang era. He'd held on to them all his life. Mom had told us once he was frugal and would do anything to avoid spending money. In the corner a few men played cards to accompany his spirit and show their support for the grieving family.

I was exhausted after my long, sleepless trip on the bus. A woman introduced herself as Tavanh's stepdaughter-in-law from Ban Huoy Mak, about 20km from his village. I had not met her before but I remembered my grandfather telling me about the stepson and stepgrandson who had left him after his second wife died and how they had taken his fortune. I thought to myself, why is she here now, after he has died? Why not come to visit him when he was still alive? She said loudly that the shaman had suggested we kill a big pig, which would cost us around K2.5m (USD250).

I told her I did not have such money because of Covid. I had been out of a job for two years and could barely afford my life in town. But she insisted on us taking a loan from someone, or asking Meuan and Thongsavath. They are farmers who work hard in the field for little financial reward. Where were they supposed to find such money?

I suggested she charge us half the price on the grounds that her family had taken everything from my grandfather and now the poor man was dead without a penny to put in his grave. I raged: "You're taking advantage of him and us by demanding that we pay K2.5m for your own pig?!?"

The argument was getting harsh and I couldn't bear the sight of her face, so Nid and I quickly left for home. We gave our last money, K750,000, to his wife, telling her that was all we had. It was unfair to load all the responsibility on us. I didn't mind helping but at that time we were not in a situation to help more than we could and the woman refused to understand that.

We left for town without joining the funeral. Meuan and her husband paid the remainder so the shaman was able to perform the last ceremony. Then the body was taken for burial.

I forgive this poor old man for all the anguish he caused us after he returned to my family. All he needed was someone to take care of him now that he was old. This is typical of Khmu culture. Your children are seen as an investment, like a pension. Rearing them means you can call on them to take care of you when the time comes.

Losing our home

Despite having moved out of our hometown in 2010, the hatred and jealousy of the villagers lingered.

Sometimes it became worse, especially when they saw us doing better than their own children in many ways. In 2019 the village chief and his siblings forcefully took Mom's farmland saying we no longer lived there and had paid no tax for two years. He demanded my family pay K6m (£600) to get our own property back. My Mom wasn't happy having her beautiful piece of land taken by those people without any compensation. It was not right or fair. She rang them, a big argument followed and finally a trial.

I spoke to the police in Luang Prabang and asked for their help in the trial since Laos has no lawyers. Two officers said they could help but they would charge K8m. However, for this amount they guaranteed I wouldn't lose the land and would win the trial. I agreed to give it to them even though I didn't have that much money. In my head I thought whatever it takes I'll show these villagers what I can do. I was no longer a weak boy and wanted to let them know that they couldn't just bully my family like they had always done.

I asked for help from a friend in the UK who gave me K6m which I added to my own money to fight the case.

A week later, the two officers and I left Luang Prabang for my hometown in one of their cars. From the main road to my hometown the dirt road was muddy and bumpy. "It's been a long time," I said to the officers. We arrived before noon.

The trial was held at the village chief's house. On my side I had the officers as well as Meuan and Thongsavath, and Phou's nephew. On their side sat the elders of the village. The sight of the officers in uniform unnerved them.

The trial lasted for several hours. We won.

The officers asked me if I wanted to fine the villagers or charge them for what they had done. As much as I wanted to teach them a lesson I wanted nothing from them. "What do they have?" I asked. Nothing. They were struggling enough already without me trying to take anything from them. I told the officers that I wanted nothing but to warn them not to let this happen again or I'd take it more seriously. After the trial we drove Meuan and Thongsavath back to my Mom's new village and then headed back to Luang Prabang. I asked the officers if they would charge me less than 8 million. They agreed to 7 million instead.

I thought everything was done, but no. A few months later those shameless people started again. This time they took my sister's house and land.

"You know what? Let them have it if they need it so bad," I said to myself. "We're not gonna make a fortune from property in the countryside like that anyway and we won't ever be coming back there again."

Moving on

At Wat Xieng Muan, as well as at school, I studied English. Being a World Heritage town well preserved by Unesco since 1995, Luang Prabang attracts tourists from all over the world. Back then Laos had no internet and whoever wanted to know about Buddhism or was curious to learn about monastic life had to come to the temple to talk to the monks and novices.

I was approached by many tourists but I had no clue what they were asking me. So, for fear of further embarrassing myself, I decided to study English, starting with basic conversation, using just a dictionary.

On a visit once my sister Lae also bought me a mobile phone and gave me enough money to pay for English classes. She supported me a lot financially for more than four years.

She was lucky to have a husband who owned an electronics company in Vientiane Capital. It was a golden time in her life — spending $3,000 on clothes and cosmetics meant little to her. From being a village girl who had left her family at a young age to working in a garment factory where she earned less than $100 a month she had gone on to a wealthy lifestyle which allowed her to buy luxury brands and plastic surgery. She never stopped buying clothes so she could look superior.

The luxury didn't last long. Both of them got into casino gambling. They lost their business and other properties and endured a brutal break-up in 2018. Lae was left with only the investment she had put into me by paying for my studies.

During those ten years and six months living my life as a novice and monk I moved through five monasteries. I was allowed to visit my family in the village regularly and my mother came to visit me in Luang Prabang several times.

I also met some interesting people. One of them

was Jutta, my Swiss friend. She came to my English class in 2011, taking over from Michael, an American with whom I had studied for six months. After that we became close friends, making me comfortable enough to call her 'my sister'. She supported me after I left the temple, especially when I needed someone to talk to.

Chris and Ken are a lovely couple from Canada whom I also met in the classroom. They added me on Facebook soon after and we became good friends. They gave me a four-year scholarship to study at university but I dropped out after a few weeks. They gave the scholarship to someone else. They supported me financially when I first left the monastery and was struggling to build a new life as a layman, before I could find a job. They also supported me emotionally.

After three years at Wat Xieng Muan I first left the monastery in 2013 to work at a hotel but, after seven difficult months living as a layman, I decided to return.

I was so confused and indecisive about my life, whether I should be inside or outside the temple. But, after more than a year of being a monk again, I decided to disrobe a final time and to live the lay life I have followed until now.

Back then I had been curious about travelling. Jutta and I talked a lot about it. In order to travel I had to leave the temple, find work and save up. I made my first trip to Vientiane to visit my sisters and made a stop in Vang Vieng on the way back to Luang Prabang. And that's how I introduced myself to a new world of exploring.

The end of the story

Growing up in an Animist family and practising the traditions of animal sacrifice and ritual ceremonies engaged me early on but never inspired me to go deeper other than to remain a part of events and join family rituals from time to time. I never had an eagerness or enthusiasm to learn about it.

The older I become the more I find it to be a nonsense, especially regarding medicine and how shamans treat sick and dying people with their magic or whatever people want to call it.

So many people died in my village each year, including my brother Sone. That saddens me. It's not the villagers fault nor anyone else's because they were introduced to their beliefs by their families from previous generations. None of them knows what the outside world is like. They're confined to a small community. There's nothing else they know of than to rely on shamans and their paid-for miracles, like voodoo doctors, that might cure serious illnesses.

Shamans often told people they were having bad luck or their souls had been taken by a spirit. Every time this procedure ended up with a sacrifice or ritual. And these cost a lot. Many families who couldn't afford a water buffalo or a cow lost their fields or their houses for fear of losing their loved ones. And as well as animals for a sacrifice or ceremony they also had to pay money to the shaman each time. Then after losing all the money and owing others they ended up losing their loved ones as well. Complaining did no good. The shamans usually told them it was "their fate. They have only been sent to the human world for this long."

I considered myself as the luckiest one in the village. I managed to escape at a young age, thanks to my Mom allowing me a pass out. Being away from the village makes many things clearer in my head. Seeing a new world, living in a different society and, more importantly, seeing how people can live in greater harmony and stick together as a community.

What was it like to grow up in a family full of violence and unrest? What was it like to face all that tension, the hatred, the discrimination? What was it like being looked down on by those around us? It was painful.

I used to say how unfair it was for them to treat us in that way. We didn't deserve it. My father Khamphew wasn't a good man a lot of the time but we kids never harmed anyone or caused any trouble in the community. All we did was try to survive, work our way through it and and carry ourselves through the rough times and make the most of the good.

I have never found a clear answer to my questions about why people in my hometown were so full of hatred. But during my time away from that environment many things became clearer. It's not just people from my village. Most Khmu or Animist people have a similar attitude. Khmu practise a tradition with little of what we know as 'morality'. People are taught black magic, of harnessing its power so they receive respect from others. Yet they use their power against the weak and poor. That's what most of the shamans, sometimes along with the village chiefs, do.

I didn't know how to forgive others until I became a monk. Buddhism is not better than Animism but its practice is more liberal and more peaceful. It's a healthy environment and more tolerant. I don't miss much from my childhood. The path I'm taking makes me who I am today. I'm thankful for that.